THE LONDON RITZ

THE LONDON

RITZ

A SOCIAL AND ARCHITECTURAL HISTORY

HUGH MONTGOMERY-MASSINGBERD & DAVID WATKIN
PHOTOGRAPHS BY KEITH COLLIE

AURUM PRESS

Text © Hugh Montgomery-Massingberd and David Watkin 1980
Photographs by Keith Collie © Keith Collie 1980
© Aurum Press Limited 1980
Published by Aurum Press Limited, 11 Garrick Street, London W.C.2

First printing

ISBN 0 906053 01 3

Photoset by Tradespools, Frome, Somerset
Printed in Italy by Amilcare Pizzi
Designed by Terry Jones

Above The entrance to the Restaurant dramatically proclaimed by
bronze statues after Clodion.
Previous page The Palm Court fountain 'La Source' with
its golden nymph.

Keith Collie wishes to thank Canon Cameras for the use
of their equipment.

This book is dedicated to Paul and Christian.

CONTENTS

ACKNOWLEDGMENTS

Although this book can in no way be accused of being a 'whitewash' job for the Ritz, not having been sponsored and commissioned by the management as a public relations exercise, it is fair to say that the book would not have been possible without the help and co-operation of the following members of the board and staff (past and present) of Trafalgar House, Cunard and the hotel itself: Malcolm Allcock, Nigel Broackes, Kate Clifford, Thama Davis, Barbara Leigh Evans, Elizabeth Flynn, Geoffrey Grahame, Jayne Harrison, Marcel Hoeffler, Jack Hudson, May Jones, Victor Legg, Robert Linsley, Drago Marinov, Bill Martin, Luís Martin, Victor Matthews, Laurie Ross, Alphonso Styranau, the Marquess of Tavistock, Michael Twomey, Philip Truelove, Jacques Viney and Harry Waugh. Some invaluable research in the hotel's archives for the last seventy-five years was carried out by Paul and Christian Vecchione and generously made available by their father, Nick, who is managing director of Cunard Hotels and has been of the utmost assistance throughout.

We are most grateful to the clients, customers, patrons, guests or supporters of the Ritz over the years who have reminisced about the place for the purposes of this book. Among those who kindly supplied oral or written material were: Sir Harold Acton, Angela Countess of Antrim, Margaret Duchess of Argyll, Sir Frederick Ashton, Lady Barlow, the late Sir Cecil Beaton, Sir John Betjeman, Anthony and Laura Blond, Richard Buckle, the Dowager Lady Camoys, Anne Carey, the Earl of Carnarvon, Lady Bonham Carter, Barbara Cartland, Lord Clark, Henry Clark, Peter Coats, Lady Diana Cooper, Fleur Cowles, Quentin Crewe, the Comtesse de Brie, Helen Lady Dashwood, the late Olga Deterding, Michael Dormer, Gavin Doyle, the late Sir Michael Duff, Ian Dunlop, Douglas Fairbanks, Jr, Patrick Leigh Fermor, Alastair Forbes, Geoffrey Gilmour, the Knight of Glin and Madam Fitz-Gerald, Lady Harrod, Sir Robert Helpmann, Peter and Mary Fleetwood-Hesketh, Lord Horder, George Howard, Dorothy Donaldson-Hudson, Mark Bence-Jones, the Marquess of Linlithgow, Robin McDouall, Laura Duchess of Marlborough, Christine and Harriet Montgomery-Massingberd, the Marchese Mattei, James Lees-Milne, Felicity Mortimer, Sir Oswald and Lady Mosley, the late Earl Mountbatten of Burma, Beverley Nichols, Felix Hope-Nicholson, Anthony Powell, Sir Walter Pretyman, Peter Quennell, Esther Rantzen, Max Reinhardt, Michael Pitt-Rivers, Lady Rumbold, Patrick Sergeant, Gordon Brook-Shepherd, John Saumarez Smith, Dame Freya Stark, Roy Strong, John Sutro, Christopher and Camilla Sykes, Jeremy Thorpe, Amber Lightfoot Walker, Stephen Watts, Geoffrey Wheatcroft, Alan Whicker, Sir Hugh Wontner, Peregrine Worsthorne and Maria Selma Zavaloni.

Of the various books consulted the following proved particularly useful: *Nancy Mitford*, Harold Acton (1975), *Lady Cynthia Asquith's Diaries 1915–18* (1968); *Gossip*, Andrew Barrow (1978); *A Romantic Friendship*, Noel Blakiston (1975); *British Gastronomy*, Gregory Houston Bowden (1975); *A Growing Concern*, Nigel Broackes (1979); *Chips: The Diaries of Sir Henry Channon*, ed Robert Rhodes James (1967); *Another Part of the Wood*, Kenneth Clark (1974); *Autobiography*, Diana Cooper (1978); *George of the Ritz*, George Criticos and Richard Viner (1959); *An Hotel is Like a Woman ...*, Willie Frischauer (1965); *Double Exposure*, Thelma Furness and Gloria Vanderbilt (1959); *Fish Cookery*, Jane Grigson (1973); *Pantaraxia*, Nubar Gulbenkian (1965); *The Savoy*, Stanley Jackson (1956); *Brian Howard*, Marie-Jacqueline Lancaster (1968); *The Diaries of Robert Bruce Lockhart*, ed Kenneth Young (Volume I, 1973); *Laughter from a Cloud*, Laura Duchess of Marlborough (1980); *Inside Marble Halls*,

Anthony Masters (1979); *Prophesying Peace*, James Lees-Milne (1977); *A Talent to Amuse*, Sheridan Morley (1969); *A Life of Contrasts*, Diana Mosley (1977); *My Life*, Sir Oswald Mosley (1968); *The Unforgiving Minute*, Beverley Nichols (1978); *Meet me at the Savoy*, Jean Nicol (1952); *Daisy Princess of Pless by Herself* (1929); *A Dance to the Music of Time*, Anthony Powell (12 vols, 1951–75); *The Punch History of Manners and Modes*, ed Alison Adburghham (1961); *César Ritz – Host to the World*, Marie-Louise Ritz (1938); *Don't Look Round*, Violet Trefusis (1952); *Gladys, Duchess of Marlborough*, Hugo Vickers (1979); *The Ritz*, Stephen Watts (1963); *The Diaries of Evelyn Waugh*, ed Michael Davie (1976); and *High Diver*, Michael Wishart (1977).

For his study of Mewès and Davis, César Ritz's architects, in Chapter II, David Watkin particularly referred to the archives of the firm of Mewès and Davis, kindly shown him by Eric Roberts, and to back numbers of the RIBA Journal (vol 29, 25 February 1921; 11 March 1933; vol 54, October 1947); *Architectural Association Journal* (vol 26, 1911); *The Architectural Record* (vol XXXVI, 1914); *The Builder's Journal and Architectural Engineer* (28 December 1904; vol 29, 21 April and 5 May 1909); and J. F. Q. Fenwick's thesis, *Architecture of the Entente Cordiale, Messrs Mewès and Davis* (1971).

Research in old newspapers was greatly facilitated by the generosity of the journalists Brian McConnell and Tim Satchell; and in glossy magazines by Andrew Barrow. Donald Wiedenman's article 'Doing It In Style' in the old *Queen* (October 1969); the late Maurice Richardson's 'A Waiter as Big as the Ritz' in *Harpers & Queen* (April 1979) and Peregrine Worsthorne's 'Putting on the Ritz' in the *Telegraph Sunday Magazine* (1978) were especially helpful.

Hugo Vickers's constant advice and innumerable acts of kindness were very much appreciated. Thanks are also due to Gillon Aitken and Angela Dyer; and to Tim Chadwick and Michael Haggiag of Aurum Press. The picture research was undertaken by Anne-Marie Ehrlich, supplementing the original photography of Keith Collie, with whom it has been a great pleasure to collaborate. Research and secretarial assistance was provided by Mary Killen, Lizzie Ross, Carey Schofield and Carole Winlaw. Finally, a salute to Denis Hart, who thought of the idea for this book after writing a profile of Ernest Bishop for the *Telegraph Magazine* in January 1974, but generously allowed us to proceed with it when his other commitments precluded his doing so.

CHAPTER

I

CÉSAR RITZ

'You'll never make anything of yourself in the hotel business', said the *patron* of the hotel in the Swiss town of Brieg to the apprentice wine-waiter in 1866. 'It takes a special knack, a special flair, and it's only right that I should tell you the truth – you haven't got it.' The surname of the waiter was, however, to become a legend in the world of hotels and synonymous with elegance and luxury: Ritz. Born at Niederwald in 1850, the thirteenth child of an Alpine shepherd, César Ritz was to spend many years in both defining and catering for the tastes of European high society on the Riviera, in Switzerland, Germany and Austria before creating the hotels named after him that serve as living monuments to his genius.

After this initial setback at the Hôtel des Trois Couronnes et Poste, Ritz got a job as an assistant waiter in the Jesuit seminary at Brieg but was sacked after he had told the disobliging sexton what he thought of him. In 1867, the year of the Exposition Universelle, Ritz arrived in Paris and found work as a general factotum in a modest establishment in the Boulevard du Prince Eugene, the Hôtel de la Fidélité. It was of this time that Ritz noted: 'J'eus la chance de devenir l'ami intime d'une charmante baronne russe.' His widow and biographer, Marie-Louise Ritz, characteristically observed in her book *César Ritz – Host to the World* (1938):

> César's initiation! And how typical of him. Russian (that is to say, exotic), titled – and charming. Only an adventure of such proportions could lure him even for a moment from his work, his burning ambition, his need for money. César had good taste even then.
> And the Russian baroness was not devoid of good taste either, for I have a picture of my husband taken at about this period, and you would never guess from it he was earning money

Artist's impression of the Winter Garden (or Palm Court), Ritz Hotel, London, 1906.

polishing floors and carrying heavy trays, nor would you suspect that he is wearing probably his one and only best suit, so elegant he looks, so nonchalant and easy is his attitude. He showed, even at that early date, very little trace, if any, of his humble peasant background.

After leaving the Hôtel de la Fidélité, Ritz served as a waiter in a workman's bistro and then in a *prix fixe* restaurant; he was sacked from the latter for breaking too many dishes in his eagerness to break all records for swiftness. Next he worked his way up from assistant waiter to restaurant manager at a restaurant on the corner of the Rue Royale and Rue Saint-Honoré. By the time the proprietor, a M. Gott, who used to feed his staff on stale leftovers and (as Mme Ritz says) was 'not a gentleman', finally hinted that he might make Ritz a partner, Ritz had set his sights on working at the fashionable Voisin restaurant. He had to start at the bottom though, and learnt much from M. Bellenger, the proprietor, who used to make the meat juices run with the fork when carving – thus creating 'appeal to the eye'. Among the celebrities Ritz served at Voisin's were Sarah Bernhardt, George Sand, Théophile Gautier, Alexandre Dumas *fils* and the Goncourt brothers; one of the Goncourts gave the young waiter a complimentary ticket to his play but Ritz found this 'very depressing'.

In 1870 the Franco-Prussian war and the ensuing siege of Paris brought dreadful changes to the cuisine of the city. Bellenger held out longer than most, but finally the menu at Voisin's featured '*selle d'Epagneul*' (saddle of spaniel) and a mercifully anonymous *vol-au-vent*. Bellenger laid in a supply of elephant from the Zoo and Voisin's became famous for its '*Elephant trunk, sauce chasseur*'; elephant blood pudding was apparently very flavoursome. In later life, Ritz and his friend Escoffier – then working at the Petit Moulin Rouge – would reminisce about these culinary hard times.

'Horse-meat', said Escoffier, 'is delicious when you are in the right condition to appreciate it!'

'A little sweet perhaps', said Ritz. 'I found, too, that it is hard to digest. But cat-meat! Now there is a gourmet's dish. The best ragout of rabbit I ever ate was made of alley-cat.'

'And as to rat meat, it approaches in delicacy the taste of roast pig . . .'

César Ritz with his two sons, René and Charles (little boys wore frocks in those days), photographed at Salsomaggiore where he was managing the Grand Hotel Termes. Here he had mineral baths installed on each floor.

At the time, however, it was far from amusing, and afterwards Ritz was to find the Marseillaise almost unbearable for its melancholy associations. Lady Randolph Churchill once told Ritz how 'beautiful and exciting' she had found 'watching the Germans march up the Champs Elysées towards the Arc de Triomphe'. Ritz replied that he had 'missed the aesthetic thrill of the occasion'. He was in fact thinking of how he could manage to get away from Paris, or at least how to earn a living elsewhere.

Ritz returned to Switzerland; as he left Paris in a packed refugee train he realized that one world had come to an end. A new world was soon to open up as the rich Americans began to come to Europe in large numbers once the war was over. Ritz went back to Paris in 1872 and was engaged as a floor waiter at the Hôtel Splendide, one of the most luxurious hotels on the Continent. His industry, energy and shrewd salesmanship resulted in rapid promotion to the post of *maître d'hôtel*. It is said that Ritz was the first to recognize that Americans had to have ice-water and to supply it without being asked. He used also to recommend the best vintages of wine as the surest antidotes to the 'doubtless poisonous waters of the Seine'.

Working at the Splendide brought Ritz into contact with some of the great American merchant princes. 'Commodore' Vanderbilt would deliver homilies to Ritz on the virtues of 'thinkin' quicker than other fellers', only breaking off to admire a woman's shoulders at a nearby table: 'Is that what you call here a *demy-mondayne?*' he would inquire, only too audibly. John Wanamaker told Ritz to 'work hard – and live an upright life'. The Morgans and the Goulds and other American families did not forget this remarkable waiter; they were to patronize his own hotels in years to come.

Just as the Exposition Universelle had lured Ritz to Paris in 1867, the International Exhibition in Vienna saw him following the drift of society. He worked as a waiter in a restaurant near the Imperial Pavilion and was frequently drafted to serve in the Pavilion itself. Here he had his first opportunity of observing the tastes of his most distinguished future client, the Prince of Wales. Ritz picked up useful points such as that the Prince liked his beef well done, preferred light meats and fowl, smoked cigars and Egyptian cigarettes, was fond of the new Viennese waltzes, and so on. All this was duly tabulated, and Ritz's sharp attention to detail would eventually lead the prince to say to him, years later: 'You know better than I do what I like. Arrange a dinner to my taste ...'

By Christmas 1873 Ritz was restaurant manager at the Grande Hôtel in Nice, and during his first winter on the Riviera he met Herr Weber, director of the mountaintop Rigi-Kulm Hotel in Switzerland, who signed him up for the summer season. In the words of Mme Ritz, his 'years of wandering in the wake of a migratory society had begun'. The particular attraction at Rigi was to see the Alpine sunrise. Every morning, about half an hour before dawn, the cowherd blew his horn and this was the signal for the hotel guests to get up and out into the snow, wrapped in blankets for the spectacle. One morning, in the middle of the sun's performance, the wind blew the blanket off a dignified English gentleman, whereupon he threw himself face downward in the snow and refused to move until the blanket was retrieved.

Once during an intensely cold spell a large party of Americans were due for lunch at the hotel when the central heating packed up. Ritz smoothly took control: copper bowls filled with methylated spirit blazed away on the long table; footstools of heated bricks wrapped in flannel cloths were ready at the feet of the guests; and the menu began with a piping hot *consommé* and ended with *crêpes flambées*. Nobody noticed the real temperature of the room as Ritz had created the illusion of warmth. Not for nothing did Lord Lurgan later call Ritz 'a conjuror'.

Soon after this incident, Colonel Max Phyffer, designer of the Hôtel Grande Nationale at Lucerne and the son-in-law of its owner, came to stay at Rigi; he was much impressed by Ritz's efficiency and noted his name in his handbook. This was to have far-reaching consequences for Ritz's career.

César Ritz's next job was as *maître d'hôtel* at the Grand Hôtel in Locarno, on the shores of Lake Maggiore, as famous for its excellent cuisine as it was notorious for the eccentricities of its manager. This erratic gentleman lived on a diet of raw ham, bread and a great deal of wine. Seldom sober, he found the business of receiving guests, registering them and seeing that they were established in their right rooms often too much for him; the number of the rooms, not to mention the luggage, would become hopelessly mixed. He once rang the dinner bell vigorously at five o'clock in the morning; on another occasion he gave chase to his supposedly unfaithful wife through the hotel corridors, trying to pepper her the while with an old Army pistol. The diplomatic Ritz commented in his journal: 'I did what I could to pacify the clients ...'

Niederwald: Ritz's birthplace in the Swiss Alps.

Grand Hôtel Nationale, Lucerne, which became the most elegant hotel in Europe under Ritz's guidance.

Grand Hôtel, Locarno, where Ritz did what he could to pacify the clients suffering from the eccentricities of its manager.

Grand Hôtel, Monte Carlo, which Ritz managed in the 1880s.

The Conversations Haus, Baden-Baden (*left*), where Ritz took over the restaurant in 1887.
The culinary hard times of the Siege of Paris reflected in a menu (*above*).

The following winter, and the winter after that, Ritz went to San Remo. As manager of the Hôtel de Nice, in his first attempt at handling the financial affairs of an hotel, he doubled the receipts in one season. His observations as manager of another hotel in San Remo, the Victoria, convinced him of the infectious nature of tuberculosis – the hotel was much frequented by sufferers from consumption – and he became fanatical about cleanliness. It was at the Victoria that he came to disapprove of the use of heavy furnishing materials that could only be cleaned at rare intervals; all fabrics must be washable, and paint should replace wallpaper wherever possible. Ritz was determined that when he had a hotel of his own, every bedroom would have its own bathroom. Such ideas were revolutionary at the time, and Mme Ritz's claim that he 'was one of the greatest civilizing influences of his time as regards this point of hygiene and sanitation' is by no means fanciful.

While he was running the Victoria, Ritz received a visit from Colonel Phyffer, now controlling the Nationale at Lucerne. The Colonel told Ritz that the hotel was in difficulties, things had not turned out as he had hoped; he had a 'gentleman's ideas of what a great hotel should be' and had decided that Ritz was 'the only man that can put my hotel on its feet again'. Ritz, to his amazement, was accordingly offered and accepted the general managership of the Grand Hôtel Nationale at Lucerne; at twenty-seven he had become a leading figure in the mother country of Europe's hotel industry – also, of course, the land of his birth.

Under Ritz's guidance, the Nationale became the most elegant hotel in Europe. For eleven years each summer Ritz presided over the hub of Continental social life: the balls, fêtes, parties and concerts during the July–August season were legendary. Mme Ritz later recorded that

> at this hotel, as early as the eighties, great ladies such as the Duchesse de Rochefoucauld, the Duchesse de Maille, the Comtesse de Greffulhe, Lady Leache, Lady Greville, the Duchess of Leeds, and the Duchess of Devonshire, actually appeared in the public ballrooms and dining room and lent their enthusiastic support to the special fêtes there which Ritz organized. In Paris or London at that time they would have preferred to be found dead than to be caught in a public hotel dining room. (But, then, Paris and London did not yet possess a luxury hotel of the Grand Hotel Nationale's class.) No

Madame Ritz in the gown of a Marquise of the Louis XVI period.

wonder these events were reported in meticulous detail wherever a society column was published!

In the winters, Ritz went to the South of France where he managed various hotels. At Menton he met his future wife, then only a schoolgirl. After useful experience running his own restaurant in Paris, the buffet of the Jardin d'Acclimatation in the Bois de Boulogne, he was offered a partnership in an hotel at Trouville on the Atlantic, by his old manager at the Splendide. Ritz made Trouville a popular holiday spot for gourmets, but this high-quality catering for the rich in a short season had its financial problems and he was forced to return to the status of employee at the Grand Hôtel in Monte Carlo, which he ran as manager in the 1880s.

Ritz took the chef from Trouville with him to Monte Carlo, only to have him enticed away by the Hôtel de Paris; he sent instead for Auguste Escoffier. Thus began the association that Mme Ritz rightly described as 'one of the most fortunate things that ever happened to either of the two men's lives'. Together they developed their ideas of what a luxury hotel should be, with the emphasis on comfort, cuisine and service. Escoffier shared Ritz's passion for cleanliness and order; he also felt that his magnificent food was enhanced by being served hot and by the quality of the china and glass on the table. The great chef later told Mme Duchene, whose husband managed both the Carlton and the Ritz in London, that the secret of his art was that 'most of my best dishes were created for ladies'.

When Queen Victoria was staying at Menton she and her 'Highland servant', John Brown, drove over several times to eat at the Grand in Monte Carlo. In 1881 the Prince of Wales reserved a suite of rooms there. On his arrival at the hotel, the Prince asked Ritz to arrange the menu: 'Something light, but interesting!' Those whom Mme Ritz described as the 'best people' now flocked to the Grand. They included many theatrical stars, and a frequent visitor was the Irish impresario, Richard D'Oyly Carte, who was already planning to build an hotel in London and encouraging Ritz to share his dream.

In 1887 Ritz took some decisive steps of his own: he married, gave up his connexions with Monte Carlo and Lucerne, acquired the Hôtel de Provence in Cannes and took over the Restaurant de la Conversation, as well as the Minerva Hotel, in Baden-Baden. The German Emperor was present on the opening night of the restaurant in Baden-Baden, and the

Prince and Princess of Wales, with their five children, stayed at the hotel at Cannes for several weeks in 1888.

Meanwhile, D'Oyly Carte's extravagant new hotel, the Savoy, was now nearing completion between the Strand and the Embankment in the heart of the London theatre district where he had made his fortune. The Savoy Hotel, designed and built by T. E. Collcutt from 1884 to 1889, made use of the most up to date American techniques including fireproof construction with steel joists encased in concrete, electric light, lifts and numerous bathrooms. The development of hotel architecture and the acceptance of hotel living had, of course, proceeded much faster in America. This was due partly to the greater fluidity of American society, the longer distances which the traveller there had to cover, and the relative scarcity of the kind of hostelries or family hotels to be found in Europe.

Having seen the dazzling way in which Ritz entertained his equally dazzling clients, D'Oyly Carte could not rest until he had persuaded Ritz to associate his name with the new Savoy. Ritz later recalled D'Oyly Carte's conversation with him at Cannes in 1888:

> He wants the *clientèle* I can give him, the people who come here, who go to Baden, who were my patrons at Lucerne and Monte Carlo: the Marlborough House set – Lord Rosebery, Lord and Lady Elcho, Lord and Lady Gosford, Lord and Lady de Grey, and the Sassoons, the Roman princes, Rudini, the Crispis, the Rospigliosis, the Radziwills, and so forth; the best of the theatre and opera crowd – Patti, the De Reszkes, Coquelin, Bernhardt; the Grand Dukes and the smart Parisian crowd – the Castellanes, the Breteuils, the Sagans; he wants the Vanderbilts and Morgans, he wants the Rothschilds. He wants to make his hotel the *hôtel de luxe* of London and of the world.

D'Oyle Carte's dream came true. The untold wealth that now poured into London from Persia, India, Africa and America helped create a new way of living that was lent style and distinction by the presence of the royalty and aristocracy of Europe. The outstanding success of the Savoy owed everything to the civilized genius of César Ritz and his brilliant chef, Auguste Escoffier, who introduced the English to the subtlety and delicacy of French *haute cuisine* and invented at the Savoy

'Where Ritz goes, I go': Ritz's greatest patron, Albert Edward, Prince of Wales.

many celebrated dishes, including *Pêche Melba* and the thin toast named after the same singer.

Ritz became manager of the Savoy in 1889 and, in the words of the present chairman of the Savoy Group, Sir Hugh Wontner, 'really was responsible for the restaurant business, in London hotels, which has continued ever since.' As Sir Hugh says, when Ritz began at the Savoy, 'it was not the thing to eat in a public restaurant, and certainly never to be seen there with your wife. Ritz altered this with the help of Lady de Grey, who arranged a club in connexion with Covent Garden, and then, when Edward VII, as Prince of Wales, patronized the Savoy, Lillie Langtry stayed there, and all the great names of that period were to be found amongst those who patronized the Savoy, a vogue was created . . .'

With the help of Mrs Langtry, the campaigning journalist and politician Henry Labouchere, Lord Randolph Churchill and others, Ritz set out to alter the licensing laws whereby restaurants could not open on Sundays and had to close at 11 pm on other nights. Legislation was duly enacted; the Savoy restaurant stayed open until half-past midnight and Sunday dinner there became a noted feature. Ritz hired Johann Strauss and his orchestra to play his lilting waltzes and brought over a baker from Vienna to supply the crusty fresh bread needed on Sundays. Thus Ritz persuaded London society that it was smarter to dine in the Savoy restaurant than in their own dining rooms, and gradually the whole pattern of London life changed.

Members of the British and European Royal families came to dine at the Savoy, including the Duc d'Orleans accompanied by his two pet tiger cubs. Ritz's pleasure when the Duke wished to reserve a certain banqueting room for his daughter's wedding breakfast was somewhat marred by the realization that the room was already booked for a military luncheon at which the Prince of Wales was to be present. As ever, Ritz followed the maxim of 'Commodore' Vanderbilt and thought quickly; within a few days he had transformed a set of dingy ill-ventilated storage rooms in the basement into a marvellous Royal wedding suite. The heavily autographed menu of the wedding breakfast was one of Ritz's most treasured possessions.

The story goes that a celebrated courtesan complimented Ritz by saying that he had 'reached the height of [his] profession – as I have in mine.' Ritz replied: 'Alas, with far less pleasure and far more trouble than you have experienced, Mademoiselle.' Not everyone, however, was

Signed tribute from the opera singer who gave her name to *Toast Melba* and *Pêche Melba*.

The great chef Auguste Escoffier (*above*), inventor of *à la carte*, whose association with Ritz was described by Madame Ritz as 'one of the most fortunate things that ever happened to either of the two men's lives'.

Artist's impression of the Savoy (*below*), where Ritz effected a change in the whole pattern of London life by persuading society that it was smarter to dine here than at home.

satisfied with Ritz's improvements and innovations at the Savoy. Oscar Wilde, whose own downfall was connected with the hotel, found the lifts too fast and did not care for electricity – 'a harsh and ugly light, enough to ruin your eyes, and not a candle or a lamp for bedside reading.' 'Who wants an immovable washing basin in one's room?' asked Wilde. 'I do not. Hide the thing. I prefer to ring for water when I need it.'

The housekeeper at the Savoy waged a long and bitter war against Ritz, obstructing him in every way she could. After enduring ten years of what he described as 'interference, criticism, intrigue, complaints and quarrels', Ritz, whose attempts to get rid of the termagant had apparently been frustrated by an ally of hers on the board, finally brought matters to a head. In the event, it was Ritz himself who left, and some people have expressed doubts as to whether this temperamental incompatibility with the housekeeper could have been the sole reason for his departure. Escoffier, Echenard, Elles and Ritz's other protégés all resigned out of sympathy with Ritz, and many of his clients, such as the Duchess of Devonshire and Mrs Langry, sent messages of condolence. Lady de Grey called on Ritz at the Charing Cross Hotel where he was staying, to tell him that the Prince of Wales had cancelled a party at the Savoy on hearing the news, saying 'Where Ritz goes, I go.'

It was Lady de Grey who laid the foundation stone in 1894 of the present Claridge's Hotel in Brook Street which the Savoy Company had bought, encouraged by the success of the Savoy. Ritz, still then at the Savoy, helped to organize new staff for Claridge's. In the course of the ten years he worked at the Savoy, Ritz had an amazingly full programme; he was involved in hotel enterprises in Rome, Frankfurt, Salsomaggiore, Palermo, Biarritz, Wiesbaden, Monte Carlo, Lucerne and Menton, as well as projects in Cairo, Madrid and Johannesburg. 'It is difficult to untangle the confusing and multitudinous events of those years', wrote Mme Ritz. 'César's suitcases were never completely unpacked; he was always either just arriving from or departing upon a new journey.' The Ritz's son, Charles, became what he described as 'a connoisseur of luggage racks'. Not surprisingly, this travel and constant overwork was taking its toll on Ritz's health; his doctor warned him, 'Take it easy, you're killing yourself.'

There was, however, no stopping Ritz's boundless energy and restless quest for perfection, and in 1896 a Ritz Hotel syndicate was formed, with the financial support of men such as Alfred Beit, the South African millionaire who was regarded as the richest man in the world.

One of Ritz's most influential supporters at the Savoy: Lady de Grey (later Marchioness of Ripon).

This English development company formed heady plans to build hotels named after Ritz himself in Johannesburg, Madrid, New York, London and Paris. The first to materialize was the Paris Ritz, but, as it turned out, the company lacked the confidence or imagination to back Ritz's brilliant gamble of constructing his hotel behind the existing façades of the Place Vendôme. The money came instead from the wine merchant, Marnier Lapostolle. He regarded himself as being in Ritz's eternal debt because Ritz had not only created a market at the Savoy for a liqueur of Lapostolle's own invention, but had also named it after this rather vain Frenchman: *Le Grand Marnier*.

Ritz's period at the Savoy had taught him the advantages of the latest technical improvements in comfort, but in planning a new hotel of his own in Paris, he did not want it to look like yet another brash 'Grand Hotel'; he wanted instead an aristocratic residence in fine taste where his clients would be flattered by feeling at home. 'Mon hôtel doit être le dernier cri de l'élégance', he exclaimed, adding that it must also be 'the last word in modernity . . . the first modern hotel in Paris; and it must be hygienic, efficient and beautiful.' Ritz was interested in the novelty of concealed electric lighting – perhaps Oscar Wilde's strictures had had some effect – and, as we know, had a horror of dust-collecting fabrics like plush velvet and even wallpaper. For the same reason he replaced the wardrobes with fitted cupboards, so that dust could not collect on them.

It seems that originally Ritz wanted the interior of his model hotel to be 'modern' in style. This might have meant a number of contrasting and eye-catching things in the context of Parisian taste in the late 1890s, but it would not have meant what his architect Charles Mewès persuaded him to have: a series of chastely elegant rooms, all with appropriate and exquisite furniture, carpets and hangings, in the various classical styles of French interior design from later Louis XIV to the First Empire style. The opening reception on 1 June 1898 was crowded with the entire world for which César Ritz existed, from the ubiquitous Lady de Grey and the Duc and Duchesses de Rohan to Calouste Gulbenkian and Marcel Proust. The Prince of Wales, after patronizing the Hôtel Bristol for forty years, immediately transferred his allegiance to the Hôtel Ritz. And so Ritz's long-held ambition of having a hotel of his own was realized. (The story of the Paris Ritz has been sympathetically told by Stephen Watts in *The Ritz*, 1963.) What more could Ritz possibly want? The answer is, inevitably, another hotel, this time in London.

The years around the turn of the century were the palmiest of all for the luxury London hotel: the idea was new and there was no shortage of clients with plenty of money. These vast buildings grew out of the tradition of the monster railway hotels of the 1850s and 1860s, but, unlike them, provided restaurants for the upper classes once the idea of eating out had become socially acceptable. The Westminster Palace in Victoria Street built in 1859, was the first London hotel to have lifts, though there were only fourteen bathrooms to its 286 bedrooms; in 1865 came the Langham Hotel (now part of the BBC) at the foot of Portland Place, which opened with a reception for two thousand guests including the Prince of Wales. In the 1870s and 1880s three more hotels were built, in Northumberland Avenue, off Trafalgar Square: the Victoria, the Grand and the Metropole. The First Avenue Hotel was opened in 1884 in High Holborn, the Hyde Park in 1888, the Savoy in 1889 and, next door, the Hotel Cecil in 1896. With its 800 bedrooms, the Cecil was the largest hotel in Europe. In 1898 came the Russell Hotel; another hotel in the same not exactly fashionable Russell Square in Bloomsbury was the Imperial, built from 1905 to 1911. More important precedents were two hotels in the smartest possible neighbourhoods: the Coburg (later Connaught) Hotel, designed by Isaacs & Florence in 1896 and conveniently placed exactly halfway between Grosvenor and Berkeley Squares; and the old Berkeley Hotel, Piccadilly, of 1901 (now replaced by the Hotel Bristol which is owned by Cunard, the present owners of the Ritz).

After Ritz left the Savoy, he was involved in the Carlton Hotel Company – which had the Prince of Wales's close friend Lord de Grey on the board – formed to manage the new Carlton Hotel at the foot of the Haymarket. This had been built in 1897–99 from designs by C. J. Phipps, as part of a large group which included Her Majesty's Theatre (just as the Savoy Theatre was built next door to the hotel). L. H. Isaacs and H. L. Florence, the hotel specialists, were in charge of the completion of the hotel, of which the shell was complete by the time of its purchase by the new company. The surviving façades of the theatre – the hotel was replaced by the unspeakable New Zealand House in 1957 – remind us of the showy, rather muddled, French-influenced style adopted by Phipps. Inside, Ritz insisted on something more sophisticated and called in the architect of the Paris Ritz, Charles Mewès, to design the principal hotel interiors, the Palm Court, Dining Room and Grill Room. At great expense the floor of the Palm Court was made lower than that of the

Lillie Langtry, who sent a message of condolence to Ritz
on his departure from the Savoy.

Dining Room with a fine open staircase connecting the two, 'so that the ladies entering the Dining Room or leaving it may do so dramatically', as Ritz explained. According to Mme Ritz, he deliberately created the interiors with the Prince of Wales's tastes in mind. These attentions were not in vain and the Prince dined publicly more than once in the restaurant, which offered Escoffier's superb *à la carte* menus at the now fashionably late after-theatre hours. Upstairs there was a bathroom to every bedroom for the first time in any London hotel.

It was in this lovely Louis Seize dream-world, set about with palms and mirrors, that César Ritz, in the midst of preparations for what was to have been the most glittering London season of all time, heard the shattering news on 24 June 1902 of the postponement of Edward VII's Coronation due to peritonitis. Ritz had been overworking as usual, planning the festivities for 26 June; not long before he had returned home early to his home at Golders Green complaining of fatigue. He told his wife: 'We might as well face it – I am an old man now.' He was in fact not yet fifty-two. The shock of the Coronation's postponement precipitated a nervous breakdown from which Ritz never fully recovered.

The following year he had a further breakdown. In the words of Mme Ritz, he 'gradually sank out of life. A dark cloud seemed to envelop his mind. It lifted only at brief intervals during the fifteen years that elapsed before death released him.' Ritz ended his days in a clinic at Kusnacht near Lucerne, dying just before the end of the First World War in 1918; his restless quest for perfection was halted at last.

And so the sad truth is that his own connexion with the London hotel bearing his name was nominal. During the preparations for the 1902 Coronation festivities the businessmen behind Ritz had been negotiating for the purchase of another site for yet another luxury hotel. Flushed with the success of Ritz's Carlton, William Harris and his co-directors, who included the flamboyant lawyer Harry Higgins, Arthur Brand, MP (a younger son of Viscount Hampden) and the Marquis d'Hautpoul sought to take full advantage of the popular demand which had been largely created by Ritz. A company was set up calling itself the Blackpool Building & Vendor Co. Ltd, and in 1902 the company purchased the Walsingham House Hotel and Bath Hotel on adjacent sites in Piccadilly; Harris and his colleagues were determined to erect in their place the finest hotel in London. The only name possible for it was, of course, that of Ritz himself; and for Ritz the only possible architect was Charles Mewès.

The Paris Ritz built by Mewès & Davis in 1897–8.
The Duke of Connaught, Queen Victoria's favourite son, arrives at the Ritz in the
Place Vendôme (*top*); and (*bottom*) the hall of the hotel.

The old Carlton Hotel on the corner of Haymarket and Pall Mall (now replaced by
New Zealand House). *Above* The Palm Court with its staircase designed for
dramatic female entrances and exits. *Below* An artist's impression of the Dining Room.

CHAPTER
II

MEWÈS & DAVIS

'At the Ritz Hotel', as H. S. Goodhart-Rendel observed in 1933, 'an exquisite thing has been exquisitely done upon a highly appropriate occasion.' The London Ritz is the product of one of those near miraculous convergences of civilized patron and architects and craftsmen of genius working together in complete harmony both with each other and with the social and architectural fashions of the day. The building has been regarded as a masterpiece from the day it was finished: indeed with the recent reaction against the barbarity of much modern architecture there are many who would now regard its interiors as amongst the finest in London. It delights the social historian as a perfectly preserved survival of the fabric of *la belle époque*, and also the architectural historian as a building beautifully put together, uniting with consummate ease, refinement and elegance such apparently disparate elements as its revolutionary steel frame and its Louis XVI-inspired ornament.

The Ritz owes its architectural form to an unusual but extremely successful architectural partnership formed in 1900 between a Frenchman from Alsace, Charles Mewès (1858–1914), and the English Arthur J. Davis (1878–1951), the son of a Jewish businessman, who was educated in Brussels and Paris. Such an Anglo-French partnership is itself characteristic of the internationalism of Edwardian high society. During Edward VII's long minority as Prince of Wales he had turned to the social life of Paris as relief from the stuffiness of his mother's court. This Gallic enthusiasm was sealed by the *Entente Cordiale* proclaimed in 1904 following Edward's successful state visit to Paris, and President Loubet's visit to London, in the previous year. At this time also, American and South African millionaires as well as Jews were welcomed by the court and certain sections of the aristocracy. The fact that Edward VII had given his blessing to this stylish cosmopolitan society provided it with a

Piccadilly shortly before the Ritz Hotel replaced the late-19th-century Walsingham House (centre of picture).

31

sense of belonging and a sense of purpose. It was the world in which Mewès and Davis moved and from which their clients were drawn.

Arthur Davis was a charming and elegant *bon viveur* who led an extremely active social life. Sir John Betjeman remembers, when he was starting on the *Architectural Review* in 1928, being sent to the offices of Mewès & Davis to collect some drawings: 'Arthur J. Davis was there and was very polite to me and kindly. He was in pin-stripe City clothes.... My overall impression is of amiability and smoothness when all was tweeds and rough rusticity.' Sir John also recalls that Davis set great store by levels and foot paces: 'All his stairs have treads which grow broader as they reach ground level.' Davis did not marry until he was 45, and the family lived in the heart of Mayfair in an attractive house which was cleverly converted from an old pub. It still stands at the corner of Chesterfield Hill and Hay's Mews.

Charles Mewès was a bibliophile with a fine architectural library, a traveller and a sportsman. He inherited a small moated castle in Alsace where he spent much time with his three children after his wife died in 1896. He was summed up in the *Royal Institute of British Architects' Journal* in 1947 as 'the best type of the intellectual and well-bred Frenchman.... His outlook on life can be described as cosmopolitan and his work reflected the general desire which arose in his day for comfort and good *cuisine* amid well-planned and tasteful surroundings with a background for historical interest.'

But behind the solid comfort and the good living lay an ordered and intensely professional approach to the practice of architecture. Both men had learned this in the same place: the Ecole des Beaux-Arts in Paris, the most influential architectural school of all time. The educational method of the Beaux Arts, based on the architectural doctrines formulated by the French Academy in the eighteenth century, was distinguished by its belief in system and the primacy of the plan, as opposed to the essentially empirical and Picturesque compositional methods of English architects. It offered a training not merely in the handling of the Greek and Roman orders and the whole classical language of architecture, but in the art of *order* itself. It was believed that what would best demonstrate the successful pupil's grasp of this rational technique would be his design for an imaginary project for a complex public building of immense scale. Each year some different grandiose subject such as a palace for a sovereign or a military academy was set for the Concours du Grand Prix

The side entrance from Piccadilly.

de Rome. The fortunate winner of this competition, which only the best students were allowed to enter, was sent to the French Academy in Rome for four or five years at the government's expense to learn at first hand the lessons of antique and Renaissance architecture.

It is important to understand the character of the Beaux-Arts education which both Mewès and Davis received, because it accounts for much in the architectural character of the Ritz. This elaborate French training was totally different from the more random and personal method current in England, which was simply apprenticeship in an architect's office with no systematic instruction on a broad front, no public examination, and no fundamental attachment to the classical tradition as the framework of order. To appreciate the full merit of the Beaux-Arts system it is necessary to realize that the prospective student had first to find a master, the patron of an atelier. The role of the Ecole itself was limited to the provision of lectures, at which attendance was not compulsory, to issuing programmes and judging the *concours*. Thus the real education came from the private atelier, so that the relationship between the Ecole and the ateliers was something like that between the university and the colleges at Oxford and Cambridge.

The Palm Court at the heart of the Ritz
dominated by the celebrated fountain known as
'La Source'.

The 'sanctuary' of the hotel: the Restaurant.
Above Artist's impression, 1906.

One of the Louis XVI chimneypieces in a bedroom (*above*);
and (*right*) stylish detail of a bedroom light-fitting.

The bedrooms as they used to be.

Very few English architects ever attended the Ecole des Beaux-Arts. A number of Glaswegian architects did, of whom the best known is Sir John Burnet (1857–1938), whose King Edward VII Galleries at the British Museum immediately betray his Beaux-Arts sympathies. A steady stream of students came from North America, in particular Charles Follen McKim (1847–1909), who formed a celebrated partnership with Mead and White which produced some of the finest examples of Beaux-Arts classicism anywhere in the world: Boston Public Library and Columbia University, the Morgan Library and the Pennsylvania Railway Station in New York.

Charles Mewès, who was born in Strasbourg on 30 January 1858, came from a Baltic-Jewish family that had settled in Alsace. The family was obliged to move in 1870 to escape from the German invasion. In 1878 Mewès entered the studio of the architect who was one of the most brilliant of all the teachers associated with the Ecole des Beaux-Arts, Jean-Louis Pascal (1837–1920). ·

In 1885 he was chosen to compete for the Prix de Rome, and in 1886 was awarded the School's diploma.

Mewès's output as a professional architect in the opulent years around the turn of the century was large and profitable, eventually including banks in Belfort, Colmar, Brussels, Zurich and Basel, as well as private houses and châteaux. His architectural practice was a kind of multi-national company which was even more unusual then than it would be today. He had representatives in different countries – Bischoff in Germany, Templier in France, Davis in England, Landecho in Spain, Prentice in South America – who would address him as 'le patron', thereby suggesting that the whole practice was run on atelier lines. Mewès was an architect of undoubted genius: his Parisian houses for the distinguished senator and minister, Jules Ferry; for W. K. Vanderbilt; for his friend, the actor Lucien Guitry in the Avenue Elisée-Reclus; and for himself in the Boulevard des Invalides, are masterly variations on French eighteenth-century themes. The same is true of his vast Château de Rochefort-en-Yvelines, Seine-et-Oise (today a golf club-house), built for the diamond merchant and banker, Jules Porgès, who had been present at the opening night of the Paris Ritz in 1898. With its impressive colonnaded cour d'honneur, it is an inspired recreation of Pierre Rousseau's Hôtel de Salm in Paris of 1783.

For the purposes of this book, the key building in Mewès's career was the Hôtel Ritz in Paris which he designed in 1897–98 for César Ritz. It was cleverly contrived behind the elegant façades of the Place Vendôme, built in the 1690s by J. H. Mansart, and so combined up to date comfort with the authentic fabric of traditional French classicism.

By the turn of the century Mewès had acquired his young English partner, Arthur Davis, who as a student at the Ecole des Beaux-Arts had been assigned in 1898 to help Mewès prepare designs for the competition for the Grand and Petit Palais in the Paris Exhibition of 1900. Davis had entered the preparatory atelier of Jules Godefroy in 1894, at the age of sixteen. From there he passed the entrance exam for the Ecole des Beaux-Arts, gaining fourth place. In 1897, like Mewès before him, he entered the atelier of the great Pascal where he stayed until 1900, winning three medals. Though Mewès gained only the fourth prize in the competition of 1898 for the Palais, he was so impressed with the skill of the 22-year-old Davis that he invited him to become the junior English partner in his practice in 1900. Together they worked on the Carlton, and then the

London Ritz. Their fee for the Ritz was agreed as 2½ per cent of the estimated building costs, with a further 2½ per cent upon a 10 per cent excess to cover contingencies; they were also to receive a fee of 5 per cent of the ground floor decoration.

The complex and beautifully organized building which arose from Mewès and Davis's designs in 1904–5 on its spectacular site in Piccadilly overlooking the Green Park, belongs both structurally and visually to a Franco-American tradition with virtually no English roots at all. The exterior represents an evocative confluence of various Parisian architectural traditions: the Piccadilly arcade echoes both Mansart's arcaded ground floor in the Place Vendôme, home of the Paris Ritz, and also Percier and Fontaine's Rue de Rivoli, begun for Napoleon in 1801; the composition of the Green Park façade with its steep mansarded skyline is a conscious echo of Hector Lefuel's influential extensions to the Louvre in the Second Empire style, particularly the Pavillon de Flore, carried out for Napoleon III in the 1850s; while the basic disposition of the façades, with wall panels and tall windows breaking through the uppermost cornice, had already been stated by Mewès on a smaller scale in his house for Jules Ferry at no 1, Rue Bayard, Paris VIIIᵉ. The arcade along Piccadilly – the 'shortest Rue de Rivoli in the world' – which enabled the road to be widened without loss of space to the hotel except on the ground floor, as well as providing more space for bedrooms, is such a good idea that it is perhaps surprising it was not copied more often.

The Piccadilly façade is about 231 feet long, that on Green Park 87 feet, and the Arlington Street frontage 115 feet. On the ground floor the façades are of a costly and imperishable Norwegian granite, and above that level they are of Portland stone. As is well known, however, these walls are not load-bearing but are simply a protective and highly durable veneer hung on to the steel-frame construction within, the first of its kind on this scale in London. The steel frame is neither French nor English in origin but was a specifically American invention developed in Chicago in the early 1880s after the great fire. Architects and developers at this time realized that buildings could rise higher, and on lighter foundations, if the weight of their upper parts were carried not by the strength of the walls at the bottom but by the steel frame within. It did not, of course, escape their attention that this implied special economic, as well as fire-proofing, advantages. Nevertheless it was some years before the system acquired popularity in England, partly because of the provisions of the London

Building Act of 1894 which dictated that 'Every building ... shall be enclosed with walls constructed of stone, brick or other incombustible substances' to a thickness, in a building of the length of the Ritz, of 30½ inches on the ground floor, decreasing by stages to a minimum of 13 inches.

Despite this, a number of interesting experiments were made at the time the Ritz was being built. These included, most important of all, the Strand block of the Savoy Hotel which was built in 1903–4 from designs by T. E. Collcutt and S. Hamp at a cost of a million pounds. The construction, in which 'steelwork was largely employed', was supervised by an American firm of contractors, Messrs James Stewart & Co. In 1904–5 came the Waldorf Theatre by W. G. R. Sprague, and in 1905–7 the Waldorf Hotel by A. Marshall Mackenzie, with a steel frame designed by S. Bylander who also designed that of the Ritz. Of the same year, and also in Aldwych, was Mewès and Davis's striking *Morning Post* building. It was due to the success of this pioneering group of buildings that the London Building Act was amended in August 1909 so as to permit the reduction in external wall thicknesses made possible by steel frames.

The revolutionary construction of the Ritz on its prominent site attracted attention in the architectural periodicals of the day. *The Builder's Journal and Architectural Engineer* published a series of photographs recording the progress month by month, and described the co-ordination of the many new techniques and the solution of new problems such as the hoisting with American derricks of 39-foot-long steel joists, weighing 20 tons each, on the long and narrow site. Space on the site was extremely limited and there was little room for storage of materials. The mortar was mixed in the basement and the stone was dressed on a platform with a watertight roof over the pavement. The excavation was begun in June 1904, the building was completed by 1 October 1905 and the hotel opened in May 1906 with the Waring White Building Co. Ltd as the general contractors. The total cost as estimated by the quantity surveyors was £345,227. 8s. 1d. of which over £15,000 was allocated to English decorators £49,000 to French decorators, and £102,000 to Messrs Waring and Gillow. John P. Bishop supervised the erection of the constructional work, and the Swedish-born Sven Bylander, who had worked for a short time in America, was the consulting engineer for the constructional steelwork which was made in Germany and executed by Messrs Potts & Co. of Oxford Street. The building was thus an early example of the kind

The construction of the London Ritz: the stone veneer goes on to the steel frame.

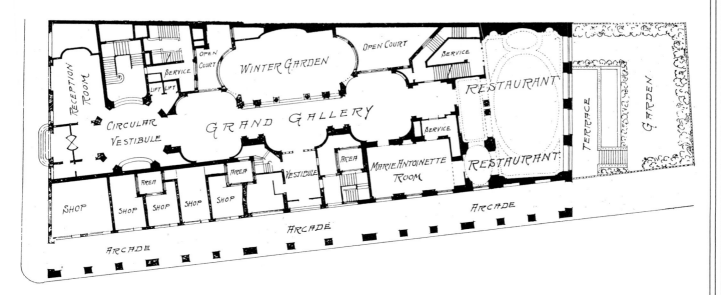

Plan of the ground floor, 1906.

Below 'The shortest Rue de Rivoli in the World': the Piccadilly and Green Park façades with Parisian style arcade and roofline.

of collective responsibility with which much subsequent modern architecture has made us familiar, though rarely with so happy a result. But without the guiding creative and imaginative genius of Mewès and Davis none of it would ever have come into being.

From the foundations upwards everything was novel. At that time the most up to date type of foundation consisted of a massive raft of concrete about three feet thick. Ironically, just such a raft had been constructed on the site of the Ritz in 1887 to form the foundations of Walsingham House, a large red-brick block of service flats designed by Alfred Burr and later converted into an hotel. This now had to be completely blasted away, because in a steel-frame building each of the great vertical stanchions has to rest on a separate foundation proportionate to its load. The foundations thus consist of a varied web or 'grillage' of independent supports made up of steel joists embedded in concrete. The steelwork was supplied by the Burbacher Hütte in Germany, and because of this the foundations were set to the metric system. At the foundry every piece was carefully numbered, according to its eventual position on the site, from a set of 2,037 drawings supplied by Mewès and Davis. Since the architects did not wish the great Restaurant on the ground floor to be interrupted by stanchions, a particularly complex disposition of the steel frame had to be contrived over its ceiling. A photograph taken during construction shows how the frame was braced with a series of 'V'-trusses which supported the upper floors and from which the ceiling of the restaurant was suspended.

Even where the steel frame carries an unnecessarily thick cladding, as at the Ritz, it has advantages of speed, and therefore of economy, in construction. The floors are constructed before the outside walls and therefore no elaborate external scaffolding is needed. Executed by the Columbian Fireproofing Company Ltd, of Pittsburgh and London, the floors of the Ritz are of steel-ribbed bars embedded in concrete on the Columbian method of double construction, with an air space for ventilation, thus making them sound-proof and free from vibration. The internal walls also enjoy similar advantages; they were of the latest American construction and consist of hollow, porous, terra-cotta blocks, finely plastered. The original air-conditioning system, in which the floor ducts played a part, was far in advance of its time – so much so that it quickly failed and has never been replaced.

The construction of the Ritz has been described here in some detail because although books on the history of English architecture always acknowledge its importance in passing, none of them contains a full account. If it has been ignored, it is as a result of the Modern Movement in architecture with its belief that 'style' had finally been abolished, and that to be morally, functionally and aesthetically successful a building ought to reveal its structure and make 'honest' use of materials. Now that a wiser mood prevails and the Modern Movement style has disappeared, it is realized that since a steel frame must be clad in something there is no reason why it should not be clad in traditional dress. The Ritz Hotel is one of the most successful and instructive examples of a fruitful union between traditional and modernity.

A number of firms in London and Paris provided the decorative work, furniture and fittings at the Ritz, though always working to Mewès and Davis's designs. The result is, or was in its original state, a series of interiors as unified in design as those by Robert Adam or the masters of Art Nouveau. The bulk of the work was carried out by the long-established firm of furniture-makers Waring and Gillow, previously employed by Ritz at the Carlton Hotel. Ritz's illness did not mean that the standards of food, service and décor associated with his name were in any way lowered: he had many followers and admirers, in particular Alfred Holland who served the Ritz and the Carlton faithfully for thirty years until his death in 1937. As far as the visual appearance of the hotel's interiors was concerned, Ritz's withdrawal meant that Mewès and Davis had an entirely free hand. When Mewès brought his ideas to Ritz, he could only repeat wearily, 'Do what you like' – a painful contrast with the man who a few years before had concerned himself with every detail of his hotels and had spent hours choosing lampshades of exactly the right shade of apricot pink to set off the complexions of his lady guests. It was Mewès's idea to carry out all the interiors with their decorations and furnishings in one style, Louis XVI. It is undoubtedly this consistency and unity which gives the hotel its special atmosphere of perfect appropriateness and elegant restraint. It is rare to find such iron control combined with the lavish funds that were available at the Ritz.

The situation was markedly different in Norman Shaw's nearby Piccadilly Hotel of 1905 where virtually every room was in a different style, culminating in the neo-Norman Billiard Room. The confusion of the Piccadilly makes the contemporary interiors of the Ritz, with their calm ordered unity, the more striking. The whole ground floor of the Ritz derives its sense of logical coherence from the *plan*, which is dominated by the single beautifully developed theme of the wide vaulted corridor running from the Arlington Street entrance on the east to the Restaurant on the west. The walls of this corridor or gallery are of creamy *stuc* plaster, jointed as stonework in the French way, and on the floor are specially made handwoven Savonnerie carpets. A series of elegant horseshoe arches leads the eye along this vista, but as one walks along the corridor, the central archways open into a further vestibule or sitting room; in the middle one comes to the cross-axis, where one may either descend to the lobby of the Piccadilly entrance or mount the shallow steps to the Winter Garden. It is doubtful whether there is any more delightful spot in London than this beautifully contrived central point of the Ritz, with space flowing in four different directions and at different levels.

The ravishing Winter Garden (or Palm Court as it came to be called), with its extravagantly sculptured fountain in Echaillon marble and figures and ornaments in gilt repoussé lead, its panelled mirrors of bevelled glass in gilt bronze frames, and its high coving ornamented with gilded trellis-work, epitomizes the elegantly frivolous comfort of Edwardian high life. The glass roof is supported by a wrought-iron framework from which hang two gilded wrought-iron lanterns, while from the semicircular ends of the room further gilt electric fittings glitter opulently. Beneath the graceful palm-fronds nestle welcoming groups of little gilded Louis XVI armchairs with oval backs, designed by Mewès and Davis and executed by Waring and Gillow. Mewès had carried out research into French neo-classical furniture design of the 1760s and 1770s, and based these chairs and other decorative features on the published plates of Neufforge, Juste-François Boucher and J. Moreau *le jeune*.

The enchanted ground of the Winter Garden is separated from the central gallery only by a screen of two Ionic columns. Descending the steps between these, we return to the gallery and continue along it to the Restaurant, which is the climax of the whole building. Flanking its entrance dramatically is a pair of life-sized figures in bronze vert after Clodion, holding gilded bronze lustres with six lights each, mounted on pedestals of polished Echaillon marble ornamented with bronze. As befits the role of the Restaurant as the 'sanctuary' of the hotel, the materials employed in its construction and decoration are of greater richness than elsewhere. The French *stuc* of the gallery here gives way to a panelled wall-lining of melting polychromatic marbles of which the names alone are sheer poetry: Brèche d'Alep, Rosé de Norvège and Verte de Suède. The elaborate light-fittings are of bronze, and culminate in the extraordinary sumptuous chandeliers which are linked to each other round the room by a chain of bronze garlands so that the room appears to be permanently *en fête*: indeed the idea was borrowed from a French eighteenth-century engraving by Auguste de Saint-Aubin called *Le Bal Paré et Masqué*. Above the chandeliers is a painted *trompe-l'oeil* ceiling on which pinkish clouds drift across the blue sky encircled by a garlanded balustrade. The niche at the south end of the room is dominated by an elaborate sculptured buffet, executed by the Maison Vian of Paris, with a handsome table of Brocatello marble supporting gilt-lead figures of Neptune and a Nereid. The elegant plate and silver-ware used in the dining room was ordered from Christofle & Cie of Paris and the Goldsmiths & Silversmiths Co. of London. The specifications of November 1904 include bronze windows at £180 each from Messrs Bernard of Paris but, in an uncharacteristic moment of economy, these were modified.

The restaurant leads into the Marie-Antoinette Dining Room, a room of exceptional elegance which can also be approached from the long central gallery. This private dining room is a glittering exercise in Louis XVI *boiserie*, with the painted panels (originally green, now Trafalgar blue) framed in carved gilt wood. At the far end of the hotel, to the left as the visitor enters from Arlington Street, rises the main staircase. This is not only a convenient position in itself, but was chosen in order to facilitate the closing of one whole bedroom floor when it was required as a suite of rooms. The spacious oblong stairwell, with its handsome bronze balustrade and its walls lined with *stuc*, leads on each of the first three floors to a circular galleried landing from which one can look down on the entrance lobby below. With its flat glazed roof this forms an impressive rotunda over the entrance to the hotel.

Each of the six bedroom floors had the same plan: a long corridor running from east to west, with visitors' rooms on one side looking north on to Piccadilly, and on the other side servants' rooms facing south towards Wimborne House. It was a convenient arrangement to place the servants' rooms so close to the visitors' rooms instead of isolating them in distant attics. There were originally 150 bedrooms and 75 bathrooms, arranged in suites comprising two bedrooms, a sitting room and separate lavatory. Each suite was shut off from the main corridor by its own lobby.

View of a suite (*above*); and (*right*) artist's impression 1906 of the old Ballroom
that was later replaced by the Grill Room and is now part of the Ritz Casino.

The walls of the bedrooms were originally painted white to suit Ritz's notions of hygiene and the beds were of brass, not wood, for the same reason. Colour was provided by the pink and green Persian rugs. The servants' rooms were painted French grey or Wedgwood green. The grandest suites were, and are, at the west end facing on to Green Park. These contain little oval-ended panelled salons elegantly recapturing the atmosphere of the Petit Trianon. In the complete reconstruction of the bedroom floors carried out in the late 1970s, all the suites save those at the west end have disappeared, but many of the fittings, including the exceptionally stylish Louis XVI chimneypieces in different coloured marbles, have happily survived.

In the basement there was originally a Ballroom with further reception rooms and private dining rooms. The Ballroom, with its elaborate and rather Baroque plaster ceiling, was later completely rebuilt as the Grill Room. This room, decorated in the International Modern style of the 1930s, was itself replaced in 1978 by the stylistically far more sympathetic Casino designed in the Louis XVI manner by Robert Lush of the Richmond Design Group. Though known as the Ritz Casino, it is not in fact part of the hotel, being under the separate ownership and management of the Grand Metropolitan group.

The original bathrooms (replaced during the recent redecoration) were tiled
from floor to ceiling.

Neptune with his Nereid presiding over the Restaurant.

The restrained Parisian luxury of the Ritz, which gave a new and wholly delightful meaning to the political concept of the *Entente Cordiale*, quickly made Mewès and Davis the most fashionable architects in Edwardian society. The enthusiasm of the rich for French eighteenth-century interior decoration and furniture dated back at least to the 1870s with, for example, the creation of Waddesdon Manor, Buckinghamshire, for Baron Ferdinand de Rothschild. The style most favoured at this time was that of the Régence, or Rococo. The 1890s, however, saw the beginnings of a revival of the more chaste classical styles associated with the reign of Louis XVI as, for instance, in the work carried out at 38 Hill Street for Carl Meyer, the first chairman of De Beers. It is interesting to see how Mewès and Davis's clients were largely drawn from the same cosmopolitan group of the very rich, often with American or South African connexions, who flocked to the hotels managed by César Ritz, where the French architectural style associated with his name shed a new and instructive light on Talleyrand's celebrated reference to 'la douceur de vivre' of pre-Revolutionary France.

In the last golden years before 1914 Mewès and Davis made extensive alterations to private houses in Grosvenor, Belgrave and Portman Squares, and indeed throughout the West End of London; the names of their clients included Astor, Beit, Gulbenkian, Cunard, Koch, Spitzel, the Duke of Beaufort, Lord Furness, the Baroness de Brienen, and Cora, Countess of Strafford (the American widow of the 4th Earl). For the German-born South African millionaire, Sir Julius Wernher, Bt, Mewès and Davis remodelled Luton Hoo in Bedfordshire, creating a superb circular staircase dominated by two sculptural groups executed from their designs by Ferdinand Faivre in Paris. The interiors of Sir Julius's London house, Bath House in Piccadilly, were also remodelled in French styles.

Mewès and Davis also carried out extensive work for other leaders of Edwardian society who frequented the Ritz: in particular, Lord and Lady de Grey and Mrs Ronald Greville. Lord de Grey, a friend of César Ritz, became Treasurer of the Household to Queen Alexandra in 1901 and succeeded his father as 2nd Marquess of Ripon in 1909; he is chiefly remembered for his activities with a gun – between the ages of fifteen and seventy, he shot a total of 556,813 head of game. In about 1906 Mewès and Davis extended his Surrey villa, Coombe Court at Kingston Hill, by providing a great saloon, twenty feet high, and a series of smaller rooms, all in a variety of French eighteenth-century styles.

Mewès & Davis's festive offices of 1906–7 (since altered) for the *Morning Post* face
Shaw's sturdier Gaiety Theatre (1901–3), now demolished. In the middle background is
the Waldorf Hotel of 1905, inspired by the Ritz.

The first-class restaurant on SS *Aquitania*: one of several Cunard liners' interiors
designed by Arthur Davis.

The Royal Automobile Club, Pall Mall, designed by Mewès & Davis and
built 1908–1911. Exterior (*right*): an echo of the Place de la Concorde.
Interior (*above*): Neo-Palladian fittings.

They later remodelled the interiors of the London house of that great hostess Mrs Greville at 16 Charles Street (later the Guards' Club). Sir Sacheverell Sitwell remembers meeting Arthur Davis at luncheon there, noting 'his air of polite astonishment when I told him how much I admired the dining room at the Ritz Hotel. Obviously he was unused to praise from the younger generation. This was in about 1935 – and it is good to think he is now appreciated and acclaimed.'

The finest surviving Mayfair house designed by Mewès and Davis is 88 Brook Street (sometimes known as 8 Grosvenor Square), reconstructed behind the old façades for Henry Coventry, a younger son of the 9th Earl of Coventry. In 1907 he married an American, Edith Kip, and employed Mewès and Davis to rebuild his London house in 1909–10. Its spectacular plan built up to a cruciform dining room which opened on to a roof garden where the vista was terminated by a central fountain in a rusticated niche. Of a similarly high quality, but now alas destroyed, was 27 Grosvenor Square, designed in 1912 for Robert Fleming. The fashionable Parisian interior decorator, Marcel Boulanger, was called in by Mewès and Davis to design the interiors of the large new dining room which opened on to an impressive courtyard dominated by a two-storeyed loggia. In 1910 Boulanger had decorated interiors at Claridge's and at the nearby Bourdon House for the Countess of Essex, another of the many Americans who married into the English aristocracy in these years. Much of the decorative work at 27 Grosvenor Square was carried out by the very able London cabinet-making firm of Charles Mellier & Co., who had already worked in similar French styles at 12 Hyde Park Gardens for Anton Dunkels, at 14 Grosvenor Square (1901–2) and at 45 Grosvenor Square in 1897 for Sir James Miller, Bt, Lord Curzon's brother-in-law. At 26 Grosvenor Square, next door to Mewès and Davis's No. 27, lived George Cooper who married an American in 1887, was made a baronet in 1905, and employed the firm of Howard & Sons to remodel his drawing rooms in the Louis XVI style in time for Edward VII's Coronation in 1902.

We should not overlook the two London clubs on which Mewès and Davis worked in 1908 as a direct result of the obvious social and architectural success of the Ritz. The Cavalry Club had been founded in 1890 for officers of the English, Indian and Yeomanry cavalry regiments and of the Royal Horse Artillery. They took over a large, rather dull classical block in Piccadilly, originally designed by A. Croft in about 1887,

which Mewès and Davis extended eastwards with a large block in similar style. Far more successful architecturally, though markedly less distinguished socially, was Mewès and Davis's Royal Automobile Club in Pall Mall, where they had a free hand on a large site. In front of a complex steel frame they provided a noble columnar façade in Portland stone based on Gabriel's twin palaces of the mid-eighteenth century in the Place de la Concorde. There was a certain appropriateness in this choice since one of them is the home of the Automobile-Club de France. Mewès and Davis's façade is adorned with crisp and stylish metalwork and sculpture by French craftsmen, Faivre, Ragon and the Maison Vian. The beautiful and logical plan consists of two cross-axes meeting in a central, two-storeyed, domed, oval vestibule in the Louis XVI manner, encircled by a Doric colonnade on the first floor. From the base of the curved steps leading to this vestibule from the Pall Mall entrance lobby one catches glimpses of the gardens of Carlton House Terrace immediately south of the Club, and also of the shimmering green water and mosaic columns of the great swimming-bath in the basement.

Much of the eclectic interior decoration was carried out by Frenchmen. On their visit to the building in December 1910, members of the Architectural Association were amused by the unusual sight of French workmen applying the *stuc*, 'dressed in their smocks, many wearing sabots and invariably smoking'. The lounge was decorated by Marcel Boulanger in a Louis XIV style; the restaurant and adjoining reception room are by P. H. Remon and Sons of Paris, and include eighteenth-century paintings in the style of Hubert Robert removed from a French château; the great clubroom was entrusted to the firm of Lenygon and Morant who incorporated or remodelled fragments of the rich Palladian decoration of Brettingham's Cumberland House of the 1760s which had to be demolished to make way for the Royal Automobile Club; other rooms were decorated in the styles of Sir William Chambers and of Robert Adam, with plasterwork provided from eighteenth-century moulds by the firm of George Jackson & Sons Ltd (now part of the Trafalgar House group, like the Ritz itself). This beautiful web of illusion and reality, assembling fine craftsmanship from different periods and countries, is woven miraculously round its skeleton of steel, its reinforced concrete floors and its porous, fireproof, internal walls. Opened in the spring of 1911, it had taken nearly three years to build and had cost over a quarter of a million pounds.

Their combination of luxury and illusion made Mewès and Davis natural choices as architects for the interiors of the great ocean-going liners of the Hamburg-Amerika and Cunard lines. The *Imperator*, designed in 1912 with imperial suites for the Kaiser, and the *Admiral von Tirpitz* were the work of Mewès and his Swiss partner, Alphonse Bischoff; but the *Amerika* and the *Aquitania* of 1913 were designed by Mewès and Davis in a variety of English and French eighteenth-century styles. When it was suggested to Davis that the ocean liner should reflect in its interior the function of the exterior, he replied that this had originally been his thought until it had been impressed upon him that most of the people travelling on these ships were doing so through necessity rather than for pleasure: 'The people who use these ships are not pirates,' he explained, 'they are mostly sea-sick American ladies, and the one thing they want to forget when they are on the vessel is that they are on a ship at all.' Davis went on to design the interiors of several more Cunard liners, including the *Queen Mary*, the *Aquitania*, the *Franconia* and the *Laconia*. He also designed Cunard's building in Liverpool and his last commercial building was in fact Cunard's London headquarters in Leadenhall Street (completed in 1932).

The all but unique experiment of a partnership between an English and a French architect was at once imitated, such was the success of the Mewès and Davis collaboration. In 1902 a young French architect, Fernand Billerey (1878–1951), was working in the office of Detmar Blow (1867–1939), who up to that time worked mainly in the Arts and Crafts tradition. In 1905 he turned to urban commissions in the West End of London and took Billerey into partnership with him. They built extensively on the Grosvenor estate in Mayfair, but their best work is perhaps the complete remodelling in 1906–7 of the interiors of Nash's 10 Carlton House Terrace. The long entrance hall, staircase and the first-floor gallery and ballroom to which they lead are amongst the finest of their date in London and immediately proclaim their French origin. The work was carried out for the 2nd Viscount Ridley whose wife, daughter of the 1st Lord Wimborne, had been brought up amidst the splendours of Wimborne House next to the Ritz Hotel in Arlington Street and doubtless wished to emulate the magnificence of her father's mansion.

As we began this chapter by considering how the elegantly lucid planning and organization of the Ritz Hotel may have been influenced by the architectural education received by both Mewès and Davis at the

Ecole des Beaux-Arts in Paris, so it may be appropriate to end it by noting the attempt to introduce a similar system of education into this country. It was in 1913 that the first atelier along Beaux-Arts lines was set up in England. This interesting offspring of the architectural *Entente Cordiale* was conceived in September 1912 at a meeting of the Society of Architects which had been founded in 1884. The First Atelier, as it was called, was opened in February 1913 in premises in Wells Mews off Oxford Street, under the auspices of the Society of Architects and of the Ecole des Beaux-Arts itself. Its honorary members included Pascal and Laloux, and its committee of management included Jules Godefroy and Charles Mewès, as well as Arthur Davis, H. V. Lanchester and Edwin Lutyens. Mewès and Davis were appointed the first joint *patrons*, and the *sous-patron* was Chaurès, who was later succeeded by Hector Corfiato. Of course the First Atelier and the whole classical revival, which was powerfully promoted by architectural professors like Charles Reilly, Albert Richardson and F. M. Simpson, and by architectural periodicals like the *Builder's Journal*, was dealt a death blow by the First World War and the subsequent rise of German architectural ideology. The Atelier did, in fact, survive the war and lasted until 1923 when it was incorporated into the Royal Institute of British Architects. The architect Charles Reilly sent his best pupils on there after they had graduated under him at the Liverpool School of Architecture, as it was intended for mature not fledgling students. Reilly subsequently wrote of it:

> Looking at the London of that time from the vantage-point of Liverpool, I remember that this atelier for design under Davis's direction seemed the only organized teaching in London one had to consider. In its short life it did great work. It changed the somewhat suburban outlook of a number of young men now in the front rank and gave them instead the direct logical French method of finding the suitable *parti* and sticking to it.

There could be no more intelligent epitaph than this on the tragically short-lived belief in the creation of centres of excellence which the life work of César Ritz, Charles Mewès and Arthur Davis states so clearly, and which the Ritz Hotel ushered in with such confidence and such beauty.

The rotunda and the staircase.

CHAPTER

III

EDWARDIAN HEYDAY

The Ritz opened on 15 May 1906 and an inauguration ceremony was planned in the form of a press dinner on 24 May. The minutes for the board meeting of the 25th, however, make no mention of the opening of the hotel and it is clear that it was far from ready; any number of hectic decisions were still being taken behind the scenes. The three-year contract with Henry Elles, the manager, had not been settled until the end of February. Elles had resigned from the Savoy at the same time as César Ritz and was now to manage the Ritz Hotels in both Paris and London for a salary of £3,200 a year. Ritz himself was given the title of 'advising manager' in March; he described the hotel as 'a small house to which I am proud to see my name attached'.

The details to be settled under the heading of 'Fixtures, Fittings and Equipment' were never-ending. It was decided not to install a dishwashing machine, the Doulton baths were to be six feet long and solid to the floor (not on feet); the linen contract went to Messrs McCrum, Watson and Mercier of Belfast; chemists, bootmakers, corsetiers, fancy jewellers, opticians, tobacconists and hatters were not regarded as suitable tenants for the shops in the arcade. The right of way in the arcade and the footway itself was sold to the London County Council for £13,844. Messrs Green were contracted the day after the advertised opening to lay the garden in Green Park which had been permitted by the Crown Commissioners.

The long-running feud with Lord Wimborne, the steel magnate who lived at Wimborne House next door in Arlington Street, dragged on for years. Lord Wimborne's son, the 1st Viscount, sometime Lord-Lieutenant of Ireland, had the better of the hotel in a famous exchange with one of the directors, Henry Higgins. Higgins, whose lack of luck on the turf had obliged him to forsake the Household Brigade in order to

Madame Pavlova about to dance at the Ritz, May 1912.

become a solicitor, asked Lord Wimborne if he would sell his house as the management was thinking of enlarging the hotel. 'And I am thinking of enlarging my garden', said Lord Wimborne. 'How much will you take for the Ritz?'

The building of the Ritz upset several local residents. Peter Coats remembers an old lady friend who lived in Berkeley Square saying that when the Ritz was built, closing the view down to the park, some of the people in the Square thought their health would suffer from lack of air.

The hotel's first sales brochure advertised the following rates:

Single Bedroom (including bath)	from 10s. 6d.
Single Bedroom (with private bath)	1 Guinea
Double Bedded Room (including bath)	1 Guinea
Double Bedded Room (with private bath)	30s. 0d.

Suites ranged from 1½ guineas to 3½ guineas; servants' board was 6s. per day. The brochure stressed that the important question of sanitation had been made 'the special study of the most celebrated experts, with the result that these arrangements leave nothing to be desired', but unfortunately one of the first crises in the new hotel concerned the lavatories. On 30 May 1906 it was noted that 'they were giving great dissatisfaction' and at an emergency meeting the following day the men from Doultons recommended that a three-gallon china flush tank be installed to alleviate the problem. Although there was an ingenious system of air-conditioning, whereby fresh air was pumped – 'at any temperature required' – from a fan room in the basement to all parts of the building so that the air was 'automatically changed every few minutes without a draught being caused', the ventilation in the kitchen apparently left a great deal to be desired and the management was faced with many complaints on that score.

Nevertheless, it was presumably all right on the night and the menu shown here was served at the Opening Dinner which went ahead as planned on 24 May 1906. Apart from champagne, the principal wines served were Moselblümchen 1897 and Château Léoville 1878. On a slightly more mundane level, the *à la carte* luncheon was fixed at 6s. per person. The restaurant was immediately adopted by the society for which the Ritz was designed; the German and Austrian embassies retained a table for all meals.

MENU.
―――

Hors d'Oeuvres Moscovite.
―――

Consommé Viveur.
Potage Rossolnick.
―――

Filets de soles au champagne.
Queues d'Ecrevisses Américaine.
―――

Selle d'agneau à la broche.
Courgettes à la Serbe.
Pommes fondantes.
―――

Poularde Vendôme.
―――

Granité au Kirsch.
―――

Cailles aux feuilles de vigne.
Salade cœurs de laitues.
―――

Asperges de Paris sauce mousseline.
―――

Comtesse Montmorency.
―――

Friandises.
―――

Corbeilles de fruits.

'And I am thinking of enlarging my garden': Lord Wimborne, the Ritz's neighbour (*right*).

The King's friend Alice Keppel, an early patron of the hotel.

The kitchens contained not only numerous Frenchmen but also a specialist in Russian soups and a Viennese pastry cook. The cakes at the Ritz were greatly prized; King Edward, realizing his *pâtissier* at Buckingham Palace was outdistanced, ordered a regular supply from the hotel. The King and his friend Mrs Keppel often dined at the hotel in the Marie Antoinette suite where the financier Sir Ernest Cassel entertained in lavish style.

Escoffier himself never actually worked at the Ritz, although he was occasionally consulted in an advisory capacity, and it was not until the arrival of M. Malley, a year after the hotel opened, that the kitchens really came into their own. Malley had been *saucier* at the Paris Ritz and was transferred to London as Chef des Cuisines. He is credited with the invention of various delectable dishes such as *Saumon Marquise de Sévigné* (salmon with a crayfish mousse), *Filet de Sole Romanoff* (served with mussels, small slices of apple and artichokes) and *Poulet en Chaudfroid* (chicken accompanied by a curry-flavoured mousse of pinkish hue). To Louis Diat (the inventor of *Crème Vichyssoise glacée*), Malley was 'my professional ideal' and he described the invention of another famous dish:

> A special party was planned, and Malley decided to add tiny white grapes to the white-wine sauce for the fish course. He gave instructions to a trusted under-chef, and went out, as usual, for the afternoon. When he returned, he found the young man so excited that he could hardly work. Monsieur Malley discovered that the young man's wife had just presented him with a baby girl, their first child. Monsieur Malley asked what they would name the child. 'Veronique' was the reply. '*Alors*', said the chef des cuisines, 'we'll call the new dish *Filets de Sole Veronique.*'

As for the *entremets*, Malley is also remembered for *Pêche Belle Dijonaise* — peaches with blackcurrant sorbet and a dash of *crème de cassis*.

Grapes were obviously one of Malley's specialities as Lady Bonham Carter, that eternally energetic presence at every social function connected with the arts, recalls: 'I used to love going to the Ritz as a girl before the First War. We'd dance downstairs to Cassano's orchestra and then go upstairs and have a delicious dinner of cold consommé, quails with grapes and ice-cream.'

The most remarkable survivor of that golden Edwardian generation, Lady Diana Cooper, who used to live in Arlington Street some years before the hotel was built, says that the Ritz was the first hotel to which young unmarried women were allowed to go unchaperoned. 'My mother would not let me go to hotels', said Lady Diana. 'Not the Carlton – the Aga Khan went to the Carlton, but that didn't matter, it was really a hotel for men anyway; certainly *not* the Savoy – that was where men took ladies. The Ritz, however, was different.' Her mother, the Duchess of Rutland, liked beauty and in her (and everybody else's) eyes the Ritz was 'beautiful, a palace'.

The present chairman of the Savoy group, Sir Hugh Wontner maintains that the Ritz 'was never a great financial success, because it had too few bedrooms, and that is why it was built over the pavement, to obtain more. Within the hotel, it had all the good taste and good manners that were associated with Ritz, and incorporated many of the ideas he had learned at the Savoy, but financially it had to be supported by the Carlton, which was a success for many years.'

For all the surface glitter and high life at the Ritz, there were indeed worrying indications by the middle of 1908 that the hotel was not doing well. The weekly takings for the week ending 24 June 1908 were £3,628 – over a thousand pounds less than for the same period the previous year, and there appears to have been a shortfall throughout 1908. Elles, the manager, thought that some bedroom floors might have to be closed due to the falling off of business. Desperately seeking a scapegoat, the chairman of the Ritz Hotel (London) Ltd (as the company was now called), William Harris, made the extraordinary proposal that the name of the hotel be changed to the Ritz Arlington, even that the very name 'Ritz' should be dropped; by the end of 1908 the board had resolved to remove 'Ritz' from the restaurant sign in Piccadilly. Paradoxically, a management company was then formed to exploit the Ritz name in North America.

The letting of the shops at the London Ritz was a constant problem and it was decided to let two of them as a 'Reunion Club'. The first set of accounts of the company since the hotel opened confirmed the worst fears: the loss from 15 May 1906 to 31 July 1908 was over £50,000. New faces emerged the following year in the shape of Theodore Kroell, who took over from Elles as manager, and Charles Van Gyzelen, who became a celebrated manager of the Restaurant as 'Monsieur Charles'. By the end of 1910, the chairman was able to report improved trading, and this in spite of the 'national calamity' which had caused the cancellation of thirty-eight special functions.

The 'national calamity' was, of course, the death of the portly, bearded, cigar-smoking monarch Edward VII, greatest patron of César Ritz and the new hotel, who died in May. Although his son and successor George V was of a more Victorian stamp than his father, the society of the 'Edwardian' era carried on its pleasure-loving way until the lights went out over Europe in 1914. The ranks of the wealthy in Britain continued to be swelled by families of foreign origin, American, South African, Greek and German-Jewish, and the influx of visitors from America and Europe to London for the season was now a vital part of the Ritz's business. In the year the *Titanic* went down, Kroell, the manager of the Ritz, was trying to persuade Cunard to stick to their arrival schedules as the uncertainty was resulting in a loss of revenue and transatlantic passengers arriving at all hours of the night were disturbing the slumbers of the other guests in the hotel.

The Coronation year of 1911 restored the financial health of the hotel and Lady Diana Cooper recalls the all too brief period before the First World War as the real 'heyday of the Ritz'. Now it was at its most fashionable, young and smart. Dancing in the underground Ballroom and dining upstairs in probably the most beautiful setting in London was a novel and exciting adventure, frequently given an extra *frisson* by the presence of that embryo Prince Charming, the Prince of Wales. Lady Diana says that some of the stuffier figures in society held out against the new fashion for going to the Ritz – an hotel was by definition vulgar – but it was the Prince of Wales who made them change their attitudes. She particularly remembers an occasion when the rich American hostess Mrs Gordon was giving a party at the Ritz for her daughter 'Baby' (later to marry a French Duke): 'Several mamas, like Lady Pembroke, stuck out against Mrs G. and would not let their girls go, but when they heard that the young Prince of Wales was going to the party, they gave in ...' The party itself was, as Lady Diana recalls, 'fabulous'. At one stage, 'an enormous gilded basket of flowers was brought in; an exquisite female leg appeared – that of Pavlova, who then proceeded to dance to the enchantment of the company.'

On 4 August 1914, Lady Diana's future husband, Duff Cooper, then an ambitious young hopeful in the Foreign Office, dined at the Ritz with Patrick Shaw-Stewart, the poet, Anne Kerr and the Earl of Essex and his

American wife. After dinner, Cooper went to the Foreign Office to hear the latest news. He told the party later that night that 'we were at war with Germany', and then 'drove round London in an open taxi to hear the fools cheering. Ringing their bells before wringing their hands, if ever bells weren't rung and hands were.'

They did not go to war till the end of the London season; for then, unlike later, both sides were gentlemen. But the civilization for which the Ritz had been built was about to be blown to pieces and things would never be quite the same again at the hotel.

The management decided that employees of English, French or Belgian nationality who joined the colours with over a year's service at the hotel behind them would be paid half their salaries in their absence. As nationalism reared its ugly head, it was resolved that whenever job vacancies occurred at the hotel, English men and women must be preferred to foreigners. In October 1914, Kroell resigned 'due to the current strained political situation' and all the German and Austrian staff were told to go. A Mr Ernest Stainchamps was appointed manager in November, but his contract was terminated a year later by the chairman William Harris, whose own ill-health was causing him to be frequently absent from board meetings.

What an American visitor described as a 'good English law' made it 'compulsory to accept English officers and members of their families at *all* hotels at ten shillings a day each, including rooms and board'. The Ritz made a small loss in 1914 and a thumping deficit of nearly £50,000 the following year; this led to the discontinuance of the patriotic gesture towards its staff in the services. By the autumn of 1914 the streets of London were dark and everything was shut by 10 o'clock at night; the Ritz soon became a shadow of itself without the young men who were being wasted in the mud and squalor of the trenches. The Ballroom was not in use and what was categorized as 'normal Society entertainment' did not take place. However, the bedrooms were well occupied and it was decided that it would cost more to close the hotel than to carry on operations.

A picture of life in the Ritz during the war emerges from the diaries of Lady Cynthia Asquith, daughter-in-law of the then Prime Minister. When lunching there in the spring of 1916 with Lord Basil Blackwood they had to wait a long time owing to the 'tremendous congestion' caused by people eating there before a Drury Lane matinée. The food, though,

Lady Cynthia Asquith, whose diaries give a picture of life in the Ritz during the First World War when her father-in-law was initially Prime Minister.

Lady Diana Manners (daughter of the Duke of Rutland and later the wife of Duff Cooper), who recalls that the Ritz was the first hotel to which young unmarried women were allowed to go unchaperoned.

was worth eating when it arrived. Lord Basil was then Private Secretary to the wise-cracking Lord Wimborne, the Ritz's neighbour; Wimborne's deficiencies as Lord-Lieutenant of Ireland at that crucial period in Irish history were discussed over luncheon and Lady Cynthia concluded that he was the 'Emperor of Asses'. Later that year she met the brilliantly versatile Sir Mark Sykes, whose uncle Fred Cavendish-Bentinck was connected with the hotel after the war. At a dinner party at the Ritz they eulogized Dickens, and Sykes reminded Lady Cynthia of an 'enlarged' H. G. Wells. Early in 1917 she enjoyed a lively dinner party at the Ritz where the company included Osbert Sitwell, then in the Grenadiers, Gilbert Russell and Maud Nelke, and Clare Tennant. 'At another table', noted Lady Cynthia,

> the Montagus, Frances Horner, Diana and Duff were dining with Edward. We flattered ourselves that their dinner was being dank and that they were envying our hilarity. Pretended to cut them, sailing past with averted eyes when we went out, but we returned to talk to them.

'Table-hopping' is thus not as modern as many imagine. A few weeks later, Lady Cynthia found a

> huge party at the Ritz: Papa, Montagus, Lady Crewe, the Neil Primroses, Lord Wimborne, Phyllis Boyd, Mrs Arkwright, Patrick Shaw-Stewart, Jimmy Rothschild, Scatters Wilson and Frances and Diana. It was a meatless day. All the same it was quite a good Belshazzar.

The Ritz was in trouble several times for exceeding the consumption limits laid down by the Food Control Orders; it was fined in 1917 despite the advocacy of its counsel Patrick Hastings, and again in 1918. 'Artie' Brand, one of the directors, died at the beginning of 1917 and Lord Lurgan and César Ritz's old friend Alfred Holland both joined the board later that year; the ailing Harris finally resigned as managing director the following year but remained as chairman. The genial Lord Lurgan used to claim that the American Countess of Essex was the first lady to smoke a cigarette in public and that by the time she had finished people were standing on chairs in the dining room at the Carlton to watch the performance; but Mme Ritz disagreed with him and gave the tobaccolade to the Duchesse de Clermont-Tonnerre who was apparently chain-smoking at the Savoy in 1896.

Smoke of a different sort came close to enveloping the Ritz at the end of September 1917 when a shell exploded in Green Park just behind the hotel. Lady Cynthia Asquith was taken to see the huge hole by the young Lord Ivor Churchill and reported that 'all the windows at Wimborne House were broken by it'. Next month she was much impressed by the appearance of General Foch whom she saw dining at the Ritz. F. E. Smith, sitting at his favourite corner table one lunchtime, was not so impressed by the figure of a well-decorated general, who had spent the war in the War Office, lumbering towards him, having done himself pretty well.

'General, you have got lot of medals,' said F.E.

'Yes, Mr Attorney, if I get any more I shall scarcely know where to put them.'

'Put them where you earned them, General, on your backside.'

In the spring of 1918, when lunching at the Ritz with Jasper Ridley and his beautiful wife Nathalie (daughter of the Russian Ambassador, Count Benckendorff), Lady Cynthia noticed Lady Salisbury, the Greys and Lord Desborough ('who, poor dear, looked in an advanced stage of botulism'). Lady Cynthia's uncle Evan Charteris had a wire from the hotel saying that important papers had been found in his room and asking for instructions. 'He was appalled,' said Lady Cynthia, 'and said your sins always found you out if you didn't tip the housemaid.' After seeing a play called *The Naughty Wife*, Lady Cynthia, Eddie Marsh and Elizabeth Bibesco 'went by tube to the Ritz for dinner and had wonderful food in Charles de Noailles's sitting room.'

Mr Asquith's successor as Prime Minister, Lloyd George, was encouraged to intervene on behalf of Greece against Turkey at one of the many secret political meetings organized at the Ritz by the Armaments dealer, Sir Basil Zaharoff. Perhaps the most sinister figure ever to appear in the hotel, Zaharoff used to prefer to stay at the more masculine Carlton but found the Ritz an impressive backdrop for his mysterious activities in international power play. Private luncheons would be served in his suite at the Ritz; he was very finicky about his food and would eat in a silence which nobody dared break.

Two key appointments of staff took effect in 1918, with M. Bonvin, previously at the Royal Overseas Club, becoming manager and M.

Limasseau Chef des Cuisines. Bonvin made a success of the job and was soon allowed to have his wife living at the hotel. In the autumn it was decided to convert the Ballroom into a Grill Room.

The war was still not over and the English Ritz company had to administer a sharp rebuke to its American counterpart for continuing to employ German nationals; a protest was also made concerning the patronage of the Ritz-Carlton in New York by the German Ambassador. The directors of the London Ritz decreed that no native of a foreign country, excepting those that had been in alliance with Britain or been neutral during the war, should be engaged in any capacity without the consent of the board.

Lady Diana Cooper observed no lightening of the mood in London caused by the *Leinster* disaster as the Armistice approached: 'both among the People and the Ritz the crowd wore the same look and talked as detachedly as they did when Paris was near being held by the enemy.' To her the actual Armistice 'so prayed-for seemed a day of mourning. Duff went to bed with the Black Death – influenza that was to kill as many as had fallen in the war, while I with my mother and whatever dull friends could be found dined at the Ritz Hotel. I could not bear the carnival and slipped secretly away . . .'

The menu for the 'Victory Dinner' at the Ritz was as follows: *Huitres; Consommé de la Liberté; Crème de la Victoire; Filets de Sole Maréchal Haig; Jambon braisé aux épinards; Pommes fondantes; Poularde George V; Salade Gauloise; Fruites de l'Alliance.* Any survivors from the holocaust of the Somme present must surely have choked over the dish named in honour of Field-Marshal Haig.

The life of society soon resumed an air of normality, as the Duke of Marlborough reported to his future wife, the American sphinx Gladys Deacon: 'I lunched at the Ritz. The whole social world goes there, prices being cheap. All women there from M. Paget to the latest tart. Balls are being given, and the social warhorses are putting on their harness again! You always said that they would never be crushed . . .'

The romance of Lady Diana Manners and Duff Cooper at last blossomed into a betrothal when she persuaded her father, the Duke of Rutland, in an unexpectedly brief interview, to agree to the match. 'Don't go upstairs for a little', said the Duke. 'I don't want your mother to think I gave in at once.' Lady Diana then met Cooper at the Ritz to plan his successful approach to the Rutlands the following day.

New Year's Eve menu, 1918/19.

The sinister figure of Sir Basil Zaharoff, the armaments magnate who had secret political meetings at the Ritz.

Nurse Manners selling flags on 'Our Day', October 1916.

As César Ritz's life drew to a close, the Union of Hotel Employees was beginning to raise its voice for an eight-hour working day; the management of the Ritz were not prepared to discuss such a proposal. Conditions for the three-hundred odd staff at the Ritz at that time were, however, far from ideal and the turnover was incredibly high. Immediately after the First World War, 380 new employees totalled less than one year's service – nearly half lasting less than one month – and only 46 stayed more than two years, only *four* of these actually remaining for more than four years. The pay was certainly not an attraction: page boys got 10*s.* a week, luggage porters 15*s.* a week, valets £1 a week, and the man who was specially employed to make Turkish coffee merely got paid so many pennies per cup. Doubtless life at the Ritz for the staff was no worse, and probably a good sight better, than at other hotels, the shortcomings of which led to the call for a hotel strike in 1919. George Reeve-Smith, the manager of the Savoy, asked the Ritz to send a representative to an emergency meeting called by the Incorporated Association of Hotels and Restaurants, and H. E. Rodwell, the Ritz company secretary, was told to support whatever resolutions were proposed, to resist the demands of the strikers and to stick to individual negotiations within each establishment. In the event, the actual strike had little effect on the life of the Ritz and a bonus was paid to 'staff who remained loyal to the company'. Conditions did improve, however, and an insurance scheme for the staff was set up with Sun Life. Despite an overall loss since its opening in 1906 which now stood at nearly £150,000, the Ritz had survived the war and was preparing to adapt to a frenetic new decade in which there was little taste for opulent Edwardian grandeur, but rather an almost desperate appetite for excitement and novelty.

King Alfonso of Spain and Queen Amélie of Portugal on the steps of the Ritz, 1911.

Admiral Salaun with the French mission after lunching at the Ritz, September 1917.

CHAPTER
IV

CHILDREN OF THE RITZ

After the First World War, the social life of the young and fashionable in London underwent a remarkably swift transformation which suddenly made the Ritz appear out of date – 'rather stuffy' as Barbara Cartland, who came out in 1918, puts it. The Brigade of Guards' shibboleth that all men going out in the evening wore white tie and tails was to be flaunted before long by the Prince of Wales – ironically rather a stickler for the social niceties in later life – who took to wearing a black tie with a dinner jacket. His friend and cousin, Lord Louis Mountbatten (later Earl Mountbatten of Burma) remembered dining one night at the Ritz with his 'sister-in-law, Nada, the daughter of Grand Duke Michael of Russia, and this striking *demi-mondaine* figure wandered up to our table and told us about this exciting new night-club in Bond Street which Luigi had just opened. The lady in question was Doris Delevigne who later married Lord Castlerosse, Beaverbrook's gossip columnist, and the club was, of course, the Embassy.'

Mountbatten and the others duly went on to the Embassy, the success of which was to have a deleterious effect on the evening business of the Ritz. The Embassy now became the vogue destination for a night out; Ambrose's band would come on to the Embassy from earlier engagements. It was here you could, if you were a girl that is (though in a later Embassy club this qualification would not apply), 'dance with a man who's danced with a girl who's danced with the Prince of Wales'. Flushed with its triumphant success over the Ritz, the club approached the hotel – whose own introduction of dancing, on the ground floor in the Marie Antoinette suite, was providing scant competition – with a view to leasing the lower ground floor. Initially this proposal was turned down as it was felt 'that such a tenant would lower the tone of the hotel', but the issue developed into a major boardroom row. Harris and Higgins favoured the

Piccadilly in the 1920s by E. O. Hoppé, a well-known photographer of the period.

Embassy scheme, which in fact would have entailed the club erecting a partition in the corridor leading to the Palm Court and taking over the Piccadilly entrance, the Palm Court, the Marie Antoinette suite and the Restaurant to boot, as well as the old Ballroom, kitchen and other areas of the basement. Such a radical move was in keeping with the mood of some discontented shareholders who thought that the standard of service had declined, the food was poor, the wine too expensive and that a change of management would not go amiss. Lord Lurgan, the Marquis d'Hautpoul and the other directors stated the obvious: that the bedroom revenue would suffer as a result of the Embassy scheme and that anyway expenses would not be reduced. Harris, Higgins and the Embassy failed to reverse the previous decision against the proposal. Shortly after this open disagreement within the board, Harris died; he was succeeded as chairman by Higgins, and Lord Lurgan, who was trying to negotiate the sale of the hotel, became deputy chairman. A dance floor was duly installed in the centre of the Restaurant. A small string orchestra used to play in the Palm Court and John Sutro, the film producer, remembers his lunch guest Hermione Baddeley accosting the violinist and asking him: 'Can't you play something *hot*?'

If, after the First War, the Ritz was no longer the hub of London in the evening, at teatime it reigned supreme – at least while, as Barbara Cartland put it, 'we were still allowed to have rounded figures'. She recalls the Palm Court of the Ritz as being '*the* place for tea. Actually the cakes at Gunters were better, but the Ritz was smarter and grander. The best spot was just by the balustrade in those high chairs looking out into the vestibule.' Tea at the Ritz was, according to Miss Cartland, 'a useful institution for the "also-ran" men: one could meet men, without chaperones for lunch and tea, so you had lunch with men you were keen on, and tea with the rest.... We'd all been brought up as ladies and gentlemen and the Ritz was a good place to go to so as to keep up appearances; even if we could not really afford it, we had to go as it was part of our lives. Tea was half-a-crown per head – pretty expensive, actually, for those days when one remembers dinner at the Trocadero was 7/6 and a jolly good dinner in Soho five shillings – but young men could just about manage five shillings for tea.'

When asked to sum up the hotels of London in the early 1920s, Miss Cartland said: 'The Ritz stood for stuffiness and standards, the Carlton was for businessmen, the Savoy was rather fast, some others

The romantic novelist Barbara Cartland (otherwise Mrs McCorquodale), to whom the Ritz stood for 'stuffiness and standards'. She herself appears to be standing on a table.

Charlie Chaplin throws carnations to the fans in Arlington Street (*above*).
After these scenes outside the hotel when Chaplin arrived (*right*), the manager
expressed his feelings about film stars at the Ritz: 'Never again'.

frankly scandalous, and the Berkeley, where you could dance all night for ten shillings, was for the young.' She remembers, however, being shocked by the sight of Edwina Mountbatten's nylon stockings at the Ritz in the early 1920s, and Beverley Nichols dates the first appearance of beige stockings in Mayfair to the summer of 1922: 'Two young ladies called the Trix Sisters appeared in them for luncheon at the Ritz, and a number of elderly ladies felt that the country had taken another step towards the pit.'

Lord Mountbatten's earliest memory of the Ritz was as a Sub-Lieutenant. Interviewed for this book a few weeks before his murder in Ireland, he recalled: 'Being very stage-struck I was much taken with the lovely Marjorie Gordon who was in a show called *Going Up* at the Gaiety Theatre with Joseph Coyne and a newcomer called Evelyn Laye. I used to take Marjorie out to supper at the Ritz afterwards; there would often be a note in the social columns about this romance of mine.'

The Mountbattens were friends of Charlie Chaplin, with whom they once made a film in which the stage-struck sailor gave a surprisingly poor performance. In September 1921 Chaplin made a triumphant return to London after an absence of nine years, during which time, thanks to the cinema, he had risen from being totally unknown to become a millionaire idol. Crowds described as 'Armistice Day size' greeted Chaplin at Waterloo Station, and forty policemen were needed to usher the star into the Ritz where the first-floor Regal Suite had been prepared for the little man from the Elephant and Castle. Later he appeared at a window of the hotel and threw carnations to the cheering crowds below. Chaplin's stay put the Ritz off film stars, but another legendary Hollywood figure, Douglas Fairbanks, used to come to the Ritz frequently in the 1920s. His debonair son and namesake remembers staying there with him. 'On one occasion in the Restaurant', says Douglas Fairbanks Jr, 'there was a terrible flap when Consuelo Vanderbilt [then Mme Balsan] passed out and slid under the table; it was nothing to do with drink, though – she had fainted because of the heat.' On the whole, the Ritz continued to avoid 'showbiz' clients, although Alexander Korda's talent scout used to have a regular table before the Second World War. But it has never been a publicity-minded hotel like the Savoy (which has its own press office) and does not publish a list of guests.

Every morning in the early 1920s, a lightly built, elegant young Armenian called Dikran Kouyoumdjian, would call in at the Ritz for a shave and massage at the hotel's hairdressing salon. Inside the building he would collect much of his material for his sensational study of Mayfair that was the best-seller of 1924. The book was *The Green Hat* and the author's *nom de plume* was Michael Arlen; he was immediately taken up by the world he had secretly observed. The American hostess Lady Cunard once spotted him in the Ritz Restaurant and introduced the novelist to her party as 'the only Armenian who has not been massacred'.

Michael Arlen, however, did not forget what it was like to be in need of funds and was sympathetic when his friend Noel Coward told him, when they were lunching together at the Ritz, about the urgent problem of raising money to put on the young actor's daring new play, *The Vortex*. Coward had thought of asking the Earl of Lathom, who had been generous in the past, but decided he could not ask him again; this, perhaps, was just as well because Lord Lathom's name figures rather frequently in the list of the Ritz's debtors – when he had his wedding reception at the hotel in 1927 the cheque was asked for in advance. Arlen did not ask Coward any questions about the play or set any terms for repayment or even express any desire to read the script; he wrote out a cheque there and then for £250, and carried on telling Coward about his new short story. *The Vortex* was Coward's first big success and he never really looked back.

For all his smart sophistication, Coward, as Beverley Nichols says, 'had a very strong moral sense' and the lyric of his song 'Children of the Ritz' illustrates this. The number, which featured in the revue *Words and Music*, was born when Coward and Nichols were lunching in the Ritz.

'Mind yer backs': Douglas Fairbanks senior and junior make way for some calor gas (*top*) after arriving on a visit to London. Senior's wife, the former Lady Ashley, is on the left. *Bottom* The novelist Michael Arlen at one of his regular appointments with the Ritz barber, Albert Coleman.

'Poor little rich girl': Barbara Hutton, the Woolworth heiress.

Nancy Mitford (on left), Hamish St Clair-Erskine and Mrs Ronald Armstrong-Jones (Lord Snowdon's mother; now the Countess of Rosse) at a midnight party given by Victor Stiebel, the dress designer.

'Children of the Ritz': *Top right* Joyce Barbour and C. B. Cochran's 'young ladies' perform Noel Coward's song in *Words and Music* at the Adelphi Theatre.

The Woolworth heiress Barbara Hutton was sitting at the next table: her finger nails were tipped with mother-of-pearl and she was, remembers Nichols, 'waving them about in front of a dish of quails.' Nichols drew Coward's attention to this phenomenon.

'Good God,' said Coward, 'and yet she still has the face of a child.'

'Cue for a song,' murmured Nichols, 'Children of the Ritz.' Beverley Nichols feels that the song, though ostensibly trivial, emerged in fact as a brilliant piece of theatre and a pointed commentary on the contemporary scene:

> Children of the Ritz
> Sleek and civilized
> Frightfully surprised
> We know just how we want our quails done
> And then we go and have our nails done . . .

The Dowager Lady Camoys, connected by marriage to the Marquis d'Hautpoul who remained on the board of the Ritz until his death in 1934, remembers seeing those 'poor little rich girls', Barbara Hutton and Doris Duke, when lunching at the Ritz in her youth. The society beauty Margaret Whigham, later the Duchess of Argyll, lived at the Ritz with her nanny (it was at this hotel that she saw her friend, the dashing aviator, Glen Kidston, for the last time, not at Grosvenor House as mentioned in her autobiography *Forget Not*, which describes their romance).

In the summer of 1930 Noel Coward met Evelyn Waugh for the first time at the Ritz. Waugh had just published *Vile Bodies* which had led to his banishment from the Cavendish Hotel by its proprietor, the formidable Rosa Lewis (or 'Lottie Crump' as he had called her in the book); Mrs Lewis herself had been denied access to the Ritz for her distressing habit of accosting elderly peers with *fortissimo* remarks like 'Hullo, mutton chops, still fancy a nice clean whore?' 'How's the old water works? Still as unreliable as ever?' or 'Hullo droopy drawers, when're you coming round the Cavendish to bounce a cheque?' After his lunch with Coward, Waugh noted in his diary that the playwright had a 'simple friendly nature. No brains. A theatrical manner.' They talked about Catholicism and Waugh told Coward he was taking instruction with a view to conversion. Coward advised him 'to take a leisurely trip round the world and think carefully before taking so decisive a step', as well as telling Waugh the story of a Dominican prior who wanted to be an actor

Two of the Mitford sisterhood: Diana Guinness (now Lady Mosley) and the effervescent Nancy.

with the result that 'he was found quite dotty in his hostess's underclothes.' Waugh's first novel, *Decline and Fall*, has several scenes set in the Ritz; its author had been a regular customer there since his Oxford days. Here he would lunch and drink 'rather a lot' with his cousin, the left-wing journalist Claud Cockburn, and Olivia Plunket Greene (reputed to be the model for the 'Hon. Agatha Runcible'), or with his brother Alec or Oxford friends such as Harold Acton, John Sutro and Peter Quennell. While a penniless prep-school master in the late 1920s Waugh would slip up to London for 'a good luncheon at the Ritz' and return with 'about £2 to last the term on', having 'bought some collars and ties at Hawes and Curtis and cigars at Dunhills.'

Sir Harold Acton, who until recently, always used to stay at the Ritz when in London, has remarked on the change in Waugh's character caused by the break-up of his first marriage. The contrast is clear from the light-hearted fantasy of *Decline and Fall*, published in 1928, and the bitterness of *Vile Bodies*. Evelyn Waugh had proposed to his namesake 'She-Evelyn', the daughter of Lord Burghclere, over dinner at the Ritz at the end of 1927, suggesting that they should get married 'and see how it goes' – this turned out to be a significant phrase as it implied a lack of permanence. They were divorced in 1930 and Waugh eventually succeeded in having the marriage annulled after he had become a Catholic. The annulment proceedings were moving rather slowly at one stage so Waugh took Bishop Meyer out to luncheon at the Ritz in the hope of moving matters along more briskly. He asked the Bishop what he would like to start with: 'Caviar; oysters; smoked salmon?'

'Yes, that would be very nice', said the Bishop and proceeded to consume all these delicacies.

Nancy Mitford, Lord Redesdale's eldest daughter, was not such an expensive guest for Waugh, who once recommended her as a nice cheap girl to take to a night-club as she would only order orange squash. Miss Mitford's men friends were not always noted for their virility, and over tea in the Ritz in the summer of 1930 she confided to Waugh that Hamish St Clair-Erskine, son of the Earl of Rosslyn, did not think 'he would ever feel up to sleeping with women.' Waugh then explained to her 'a lot about sexual shyness in men'. Hamish Erskine's sister, Mary, was once observed by their father, the Earl of Rosslyn, to be lunching at the Ritz with what the latter described as a 'terrible old man'. In fact it was Waugh's friend John Sutro heavily disguised by Clarksons, the theatrical costumiers, in a grey wig and a false beard. Miss Mitford found that the Ritz 'before lunch is a party where you see everybody you've ever known'. Once when lunching there with John Betjeman, she took exception to his shirt and asked him where on earth he had got it; 'It came in the wash', was the young poet's reply.

Just before he met Noel Coward, Waugh decided to give 'an amusing luncheon party at the Ritz but there was a horse-race that day and everybody chucked.' In the event the guests included F. E. Smith's eccentric daughter, Eleanor; Sacheverell Sitwell; Frank Pakenham (later the Earl of Longford); Harold Acton's brother William; the novelist's old enemy Cecil Beaton, who is said never to have fully recovered from the effects of the drawing pins put on his seat by Waugh when they were schoolboys; Nancy Mitford and her sister Diana, then married to the poet Bryan Guinness. 'Luncheon was delicious', noted Waugh.

Sir Frederick Ashton remembers that Rudolf Kommer, the associate of Reinhardt who produced *The Miracle* in which Lady Diana Cooper scored such a sensation as the Virgin Mary, used to have a regular table in the Restaurant for all the beautiful women around. A frequent guest at his *stammtisch* at the Ritz was Diana Guinness, who found Kommer 'fat, bald, clever and kind'. She once asked him why he had '*aus Cernowitz*' engraved on his visiting card, as he did not live there. 'No,' he replied, 'but in America they always say "Kommer? That lousy Jew from Cernowitz?" So I put it on my card.'

Diana Guinness married Sir Oswald Mosley later in the 1930s. Sir Oswald's first wife, the daughter of Lord Curzon, had imagined that he had 'run out at the last moment' when she arrived for her wedding in the Chapel Royal in the spring of 1920 to find him notable by his absence. Mosley was in fact 'lunching too happily at the Ritz with an old Sandhurst and Army friend, who was my best man', when he was buttonholed by Lady Cunard. 'Were you not being married five minutes ago?' she inquired. The bridegroom and best man then jumped up and 'hurried hatless down St James's Street' to find the bride waiting with her father. Showing commendable restraint, Curzon 'said not a word.'

Evelyn Waugh's other lunchtime companions that same summer of 1930 included the delightful writer Lord David Cecil; they talked about love – 'I think', added Waugh in his diary. The widow of Lord David's fellow Oxford don, Sir Roy Harrod, thinks that the subject and the place are intertwined: 'all my romantic attachments were made at the Ritz.'

Billa Harrod, an indefatigable conservationist, was a friend of Nancy Mitford's and used to go to the Ritz with Mark Ogilvie-Grant, Hamish St Clair-Erskine and others. She has continued to go there for the last fifty years: 'It's the only place where I can ever think of meeting people . . .'

Many would echo that sentiment. 'Of course the *faux-Louis* foyers have been for my generation the equivalent of "Under the Biltmore clock" for Americans', says Alastair Forbes. 'The little fountain at the Ritz is a good place to meet', wrote Cyril Connolly to his friend Noel Blakiston in 1926, '. . . it involves no capital.' Connolly was a keen patron of the Ritz and prided himself on knowing the place inside out, although Anthony Powell recalls that on one occasion when the critic was showing off his knowledge of the Ritz's geography to some friends, he became hopelessly lost and ended up in some broom cupboard. In the third volume of Powell's great novel *A Dance to the Music of Time*, the narrator Nicholas Jenkins arranges to meet the poet Mark Members at the Ritz one evening and, while waiting for him to turn up, surrounded by South Americans, he muses on the golden nymph in the Palm Court:

> Away on her pinnacle, the nymph seemed at once a member of this Latin family party, and yet at the same time morally separate from them: an English girl, perhaps, staying with relations possessing business interests in South America, herself in love for the first time after a visit to some neighbouring estancia. Now she had strayed away from her hosts to enjoy delicious private thoughts in peace while she examined the grimacing face of the river-god carved in stone on the short surface of the wall by the grotto. Pensive, quite unaware of the young tritons violently attempting to waft her way from the fountain by sounding their conches at full blast, she gazed full of wonder that no crystal stream gushed from the water-god's contorted jaws. Perhaps in such a place she expected a torrent of champagne. Although stark naked, the nymph looked immensely respectable; less provocative, indeed, than some of the fully dressed young women seated below her

Several novelists have used the Ritz in their work. Firbank, for instance, has a running joke about there being 'fleas in the Ritz'. Michael Arlen's novel, *Piracy*, contains a fantasy of a revolution in London in

An intimate corner of the Palm Court, in Louis XVI style.

which the 'New Gentlemen' storm the hotel, 'a very stout and solid building in the manner of the old Bastille, originally conceived no doubt with a fearful eye on class prejudice.' The siege was 'long and bloody, as of course it would be', but the besieged

had something of the advantage for they were led by the men of White's, the most gallant of all those who asserted their right to be gentlemen when and how they pleased; and were, moreover, greatly assisted by their exact knowledge of every corner of the building, which was of course known to the New Gentlemen only from passing buses or from the Green Park on Sunday afternoons.

It was not the New Gentlemen who invaded the hotel but some of the Jarrow hunger marchers; today such a protest would have taken place at the Houses of Parliament but at that time the Ritz was seen as the target. Barbara Cartland was having tea in the Palm Court and is able to give an eye-witness account of what happened when the marchers came into the Ritz: 'The poor things were in rags; they looked tired and exhausted. They didn't make a sound; they just gazed around in disbelief, overwhelmed by the fountain, the opulence, the atmosphere. The people having tea just sat there, still, looking upper-class; nothing was said. There was an uncanny silence. Then the marchers were politely asked to leave, which they did without any fuss or bother.' Recalling the deprivation that some people had to suffer in the 1930s Miss Cartland

The Jarrow hunger marchers arrive in London *en route* for the Ritz.

paused, and then said, with considerable dramatic effect: 'We deserve everything we get from the unions now, quite frankly, everything we get.'

The General Strike of 1926 had coincided with an unsettling time for the Ritz as various new hotels were being built, providing many more bedrooms in the capital. Taxation had risen sharply since 1918, and continued to rise; the 1920s saw the destruction of the great London mansions like Devonshire House, Grosvenor House and Dorchester House. The competition from the new hotels, the Dorchester and Grosvenor House, was expected to be fierce and the major overhaul of Piccadilly in the late 1920s when the street was relaid caused a disturbance that many guests of the Ritz found intolerable. The year 1929 was said to be a difficult one for trading 'due to the severe winter and the critical illness of His Majesty The King'.

As the effects of the depression began to sink in there was inevitably a very serious drop in business at the Ritz, and in the summer of 1931 staff wages were reduced. In an attempt to cheer people up, dancing in the Restaurant was tried again, this time under the baton of Lord Vivian's son, Anthony, the brother of Lady Weymouth. The Tony Vivian Band's engagement only lasted a month in spite of his offer to continue playing for a reduced fee. Times were hard and the cashier who was imprudent enough to cash a cheque for £100 given to him by a Mme de Toledo was required to repay the debt at a rate of £4 per month. The free supplies of staff beer were stopped to all save those who worked in the kitchen and the directors themselves took a 25 per cent cut in their fees. This year – 1931 – was the most trying and difficult yet experienced by the Ritz, and the slump in the United States resulted in a serious reduction of American visitors.

Lord Lurgan, who had become chairman of the Ritz on the death of Harry Higgins in 1928, did his best to drum up the American clientele. He encouraged the Earl of Carnarvon and his American wife, the former Catherine Wendell, in this endeavour; one of their triumphs was when an American couple known to the Carnarvons took the whole second floor of the hotel to accommodate their friends and relations. The octogenarian Lord Carnarvon, sportsman, *bon viveur* and author of some lively memoirs, is the doyen of the Ritz's clients. 'The Ritz has been my London home for over fifty years', he says. 'I'm very fond of the place; nobody knows it better. In 1924, Billy Lurgan said that as I and my wife knew everybody, particularly in America, we could stay at the Ritz as

guests of the hotel and tell all and sundry of our pals to come and stay there.' Another peer was less fortunate than the colourful Carnarvon: when he was shown the various suites and it was pointed out that they overlooked the park, he replied that he would prefer one that overlooked the rent, but the hint was not taken.

'My arrangement with the Ritz went along as merrily as a marriage bell until the death of Lord Lurgan in 1937,' continued Lord Carnarvon, 'then the management said they would have to make a charge, though I had a slight reduction for old times' sake.' Lord Carnarvon has always brought a racy, old-world rakishness to the Ritz, and he recalls some of the personalities from the turf, the stage and from the United States whom he has seen in the hotel: celebrities such as Count Selern, Charles Kinsky, Paul Nelke, Lord Queenborough (father of the obese, chocolate-guzzling Dorothy Paget 'who hated the smell of a man'), Fred Darling ('the best trainer there ever was'), Ambrose Clarke, George Widener, William Woodward and Gerald du Maurier, 'who told me that the secret of acting was to be yourself'.

Among Lord Carnarvon's favourite co-residents was that giant of the turf, the Aga Khan, who had a suite at the Ritz for over forty years. 'A message will always reach me at the Ritz in London' he used to say, and the hotel became his permanent headquarters in London. His suite was decorated with roses and azaleas, whether he was in residence or not; when he was there he gave private parties at which the entertainers ranged from Nijinsky to John McCormack. Every morning Topper the Jermyn Street barber would come to shave the Aga Khan, who would then take his daily exercise in an attempt to keep his figure to reasonable proportions, either by pummelling his punchball (sometimes a human sparring partner) or by jogging up the suitably named Constitution Hill before returning to meditate and read the Koran. His widespread interests on the turf were largely handled by the porter at the Ritz, George, whose financial dealings on behalf of the Aga Khan did not always meet with the approval of the Ritz management. The Aga Khan was a generous man: 'He never *gave* you money,' a barman recalled, 'he asked you to accept a little gift almost as if you were doing him a kindness.'

In 1931, the Aga Khan played a prominent part behind the scenes in the Round Table Conference when he greeted the unlikely figure of Mahatma Gandhi, in his familiar loincloth, at the door of the Ritz. They talked about the future of India: 'We discussed our differences and it was

Derby night menu, 1938 (*above*); and (*right*) the Aga Khan and Mahatma Gandhi at the Ritz during the Round Table Conference of March 1931.

a most friendly meeting', said Gandhi, who attended a garden party a few days later at Buckingham Palace at which Queen Mary removed her lorgnettes from their holster to inspect this ascetic apparition. The Aga Khan took his spiritual responsibilities seriously and once took over the Palm Court to receive a delegation of his followers. Dressed in the traditional turban and silk robes, he was observing the disciples who were kissing the carpet at his feet when he noticed something; seizing one of the men by the collar, he lifted him to his feet and said: 'He is not an Ismaili, but a trespasser who is here to make trouble. Have him ejected immediately.'

The Aga Khan was very fond of ice cream and for breakfast used to eat green figs and mangoes, which had to be shipped specially to him. Another legendary Ritz figure, Calouste Gulbenkian, whose exotic son Nubar later became even more of an institution at the hotel, preferred to start the day with raw lettuce and took his meals at strange hours. Gulbenkian senior insisted on bringing his own chef and kitchen staff to the Ritz; this was not so much because the food at the Ritz was bad, which it was, but because 'Mr Five Per Cent' (as he was known because of his holding in British Petroleum) thought that someone might try to poison him. When Lord Clark, who considers Gulbenkian to have been 'undoubtedly one of the most formidable human beings I have ever encountered', commented on the excellence of a meal they had eaten together at the Ritz, Gulbenkian replied: 'I bring my own cook. He is a Turk. I can trust him.'

This naturally did not please the Ritz chef, M. Avignon, who had succeeded Escoffier's protégé, M. Herbodeau, in 1928, and, discovering that Gulbenkian had a weakness for saddle of mutton and Irish stew, he slowly weaned him away from his private staff before the multi-millionaire developed an addiction to uncooked fruit and vegetables. In Lord Carnarvon's view, the popular M. Avignon could be 'a great chef but he was a bit lazy'. He once told Lord Carnarvon: 'If only I had clean modern kitchens and there were no rats or mice and if I had a decent staff, I could really do something here.' Small, plump, sleek and humorous, Avignon liked to tell the story of his arrival in London on a cold November night: it was a real 'pea-souper' and the Frenchman vowed that he would not stay here with this fog – 'it'll kill me . . .'; but he did stay and was Chef des Cuisines for twenty-seven years, coming to love London. Many clients used to seek him out, not least for take-away portions of his special cheese, *le Fromage de Monsieur*.

The great Escoffier was in low water financially after the First World War, and from 1924 the Ritz board contributed to a pension fund for him; he died in Monte Carlo in 1935. His friend and biographer, Herbodeau, took over from Limasseau at the London Ritz in 1922 and was transferred to the Carlton six years later. The Restaurant manager in the 1930s was Aletto, another popular and much-mimicked character. Once the late Earl of Wharncliffe, an ardent Ritz supporter though not always the swiftest of payers, ordered plovers' eggs when they were out of season. Aletto assured him that he had done his best to procure them: 'My Lord, I've been down to zee *country*, I have looked everywhere for zeese eggs, I have climbed zee *trees* to find zeese eggs, but no, I could not find zeese eggs *anywhere*.'

Bonvin, the hotel manager who had shaped so well after the war, died suddenly in 1921 and was succeeded by J. S. Walters. Walters was a tireless salesman of the Ritz's good name both on the Continent and in Britain, and introduced new illustrated booklets to the propaganda ammunition. The *Tatler*, however, was not regarded as good publicity; in 1933 it was deemed 'undesirable' for the Ritz to appear in the magazine (until recently it was indirectly associated with the hotel through Trafalgar House's shareholding).

The finances of the Ritz were very problematical in the years between the wars, and a hefty debenture of £130,000 was touched from the Carlton in 1930. Apart from the inevitable reaction to the worldwide depression, there were other factors such as 'the reduction in the sales of alcoholic beverages' (1932). Christopher Sykes, the biographer of Evelyn Waugh, recalls that the Ritz management approached his great-uncle Fred Cavendish-Bentinck, father of the present nonagenarian Duke of Portland, to see if he could help them out with advice. The truth was that even if every room were occupied, which it was not, and every table booked, which it was not, the hotel would still not have been making money.

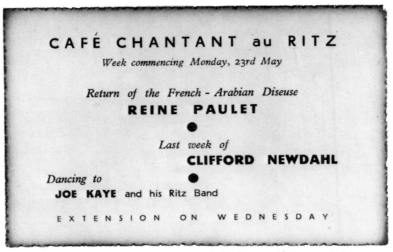

Cavendish-Bentinck recommended that a Cabaret be put on, and this was duly introduced into the dinner and supper programme in 1935. The show was advertised in the *Evening Standard* (another publication now related to the Ritz through Trafalgar House) and the entertainers included Vic Oliver, the Austrian comedian, who was booked for two weeks at the beginning of 1936 at £75 per week and became Winston Churchill's son-in-law later that year, as well as a newcomer called Cyril Fletcher on only £25 per week for a month's engagement in 1937. In the same year the BBC began regular broadcasts from the Ritz Restaurant featuring Joe Kaye's Dance Band; these helped to popularize Irving Berlin's song 'Puttin' on the Ritz' – later recorded by Fred Astaire, Judy Garland and others. Billy Milton was once the star pianist in the Ritz Cabaret and remembers that for the Ascot gala nights 'there were hostesses like Chick Barnes, the piano heiress, and my very dear friend Lady Doverdale. I met her in the chorus of *Bitter Sweet* on Broadway when she was a pretty little Australian dancer called Audrey Pointing. "Billy, darling," she'd say, "the only thing I loathe at the Ritz is afternoon tea. That blasted fountain has me running to the loo for hours."'

Earlier in the 1930s the resident bandleader at Ciro's Club in Bond

'See that he doesn't get into any mischief', said Lady Furness (*above*) to Mrs Simpson at the Ritz.

Café society: Edward VIII and Mrs Simpson.

John Sutro, the film producer, and Princess Natalie Paley at a party given by Cecil Beaton, 1934.

Street, Tommy Kinsman, took up an engagement at the Ritz and launched himself on a career as the darling of society. The Prince of Wales returned to the Ritz in order to dance to Kinsman and his band, inviting the popular bandleader to his table. The *Evening News* gushed about the Prince's prowess on the dance floor, though it coyly managed to avoid naming 'one of those hotels that overlook the Green Park' to whose restaurant the Prince had come 'with a small intimate party';

> The Prince of Wales never misses an opportunity to raise the standard of his dancing ... He danced three tangoes each of which lasted about thirty-five minutes! Of course the band went on playing as long as the Prince and his partner remained on the floor. Half-hour spells of tangoes three times running must be something of a record for the West End. Each tango lasts normally about four minutes.

That was in 1932; in January 1934 the Prince of Wales's mistress, the American Lady Furness, decided to make a trip to the United States. In her book *Double Exposure*, Lady Furness tells how she had lunch at the Ritz with her friend Mrs Ernest Simpson on the day before she sailed. On hearing of Lady Furness's forthcoming absence from the scene, Mrs Simpson said: 'Oh, Thelma, the little man is going to be so lonely.'

'Well, dear,' replied Lady Furness, 'you look after him while I'm away. See that he doesn't get into any mischief.'

As Lady Furness noted sarcastically in her memoirs: 'It was later evident that Wallis took my advice all too literally.'

In the same year the Prince's brother, the Duke of Kent, married Princess Marina of Greece and Denmark and the Ritz erected scaffolding in the garden for the occasion. Sir Cecil Beaton recalled, shortly before he died, that the pianist Edyth Baker was greatly upset by being what she regarded as jilted by Prince George; instead of crying alone in her room Miss Baker chose to make a public display of her unhappiness, tedious through repetition, in the Rivoli Bar at the Ritz.

Lord Mountbatten was not such a familiar sight in the Ritz in the 1930s as he had been in the 1920s because in the latter years he was away in the Navy. There was a farewell party in his wife's honour at the Ritz in 1931 when they went off to Malta for two years; most of the guests were invited by telephone at the last moment. When they returned, they tended to prefer Claridge's. In Lord Mountbatten's view 'Claridge's outstripped the Ritz as a "Royal" hotel because, I suppose, the Ritz was palatial and had that certain aura, and, after all most Royal Families have quite enough of palaces so they rather like the more "family" atmosphere of Claridge's . . . I remember my brother-in-law, Prince Andrew of Greece and Denmark (Prince Philip's father), staying there, though.'

The Queen Mother used to go to the Ritz before the war – she still goes to the occasional private party there – and it was here that she is said to have ordered a meal from a menu for the first time. A monarch who liked to indulge in more unusual non-Royal activities was King Boris of Bulgaria, a fanatical railway engine enthusiast. Early one morning, after he had driven a night express into Euston, he arrived at the Ritz where he was stopped by George, who was to become head porter on the retirement of the original incumbent, the awesome Schmid, in 1939. 'You can't come in here, this is the guests' entrance. If you want the coal shute, it's farther down', said the porter to the grime-covered King.

The visit of King Carol of Roumania to England at the end of the 1930s was recorded in Robert Bruce Lockhart's diaries. Bruce Lockhart went to see Proust's old friend Princess Marthe Bibesco at the Ritz to discuss Roumanian affairs and she hoped that 'someone like the Pembrokes will ask him to shoot so that he can see something of English country life.' The Roumanian Minister, Grigorcea (known as 'The White Slug') gave a press lunch at the Ritz in connexion with King Carol's visit.

King Carol and Crown Prince Michael of Roumania during their visit to London, November 1938.

It is said that Queen Marie of Roumania used to send her bills for parties at the Ritz to George V for him to pay.

The 1937 Coronation procession of George VI did not pass by the Ritz and the International Exhibition in Paris drew visitors away from London; business at the hotel in the late 1930s was less than brisk. Bracewell Smith, MP, managing director of the Park Lane Hotel in Piccadilly and a director of the Café Royal, was at this time deputy to the chairman of the Ritz, James Stephens, who had succeeded Lord Lurgan; and another new director was Baron Phyffer d'Altinhosen, the son of César Ritz's benefactor at Lucerne. The Baron was also chairman of the Ritz in Paris and had been on the board of the Ritz Hotel Development Company since 1910. In 1938 the new board rejected a request made by the House of Lords that the Ritz should take over its catering.

In the same year members of the Travellers' Club were given a 20 per cent discount on meals taken in the Grill Room at the Ritz for a trial period. Robin McDouall, the culinary writer who was to be a distinguished secretary of the Travellers' after the Second World War, remembers dining in the Grill occasionally with Barbara Cartland's brother, Ronnie. The food was straightforward enough and, in any event, Cartland (later killed in action) insisted on '"a gentleman's meal": say, *oeuf en cocotte*; lamb cutlets and mushrooms on toast.' McDouall never thought of the Ritz as being particularly chic between the wars and Lady Diana Cooper felt that it reached a low ebb in the 1930s.

Sir Michael Duff, however, looked back 'with great love and nostalgia to those halcyon days of the Ritz before the last war'. Shortly before his death he told us that the hotel was 'very much part of my daily life when I was in London in my early days in the 1930s. It had a special atmosphere about it and the Palm Court was always filled before luncheon with "society beauties", debutantes and their boy friends, and famous actors and actresses – though the latter seldom seemed to actually lunch there. Bejewelled American ladies used to parade up and down the corridor awaiting their guests. The Ritz was more like a club than an hotel; you were bound to see your friends there. To "meet at the Ritz" was the obvious choice. It had the combination of elegance and cosiness. The Ritz had an essentially happy atmosphere which radiated from the staff. All the waiters knew everybody and became personal friends. The Ritz in those days had a courtesy and elegance unlike any other hotel; it was thought of as "home" in a sense that never applied to anywhere else.'

CHAPTER
V

THE SECOND WAR

At ten o'clock one evening in the late summer of 1939, the young night switchboard operator at the Ritz put through a call for Randolph Churchill, who was in the bar, to the Grill Room and overheard the following dialogue:

'Randy?'

'Yes.'

'German Army marches tomorrow morning, nine o'clock.'

The outbreak of the Second World War caused the Ritz board to declare the future trading position 'uncertain'. Three days after Chamberlain had declared 'we are at war with Germany', it was decided to close the Grill Room for lunch and the Restaurant for dinner and supper, due to the 'very poor business'.

But the management had not taken into account the points which that shrewd observer of the way of the world, 'Chips' Channon, noted in his diary later that month: 'Ritzes always thrive in wartime, as we are all cookless. Also in wartime the herd instinct rises . . .' On the same day, Channon lunched at the Ritz with his wife, her sister Lady Brigid Guinness (who was to marry the Kaiser's grandson after the war) and Harold Balfour. He saw that the Ritz had become 'fantastically fashionable; all the great, gay, the Government; we knew 95 per cent of everyone there'. One evening a few weeks later Channon noticed, over cocktails: 'The Dukes of Marlborough (who calls his wife, who is in uniform, the General), Northumberland and Leeds, more like a pekinese than ever. It was "The Dukeries" in excelsis'. In the same month Evelyn Waugh, just about to be called up into the Royal Marines, found the Churchill family having drinks before luncheon at the Ritz. Waugh was lunching with Henry Yorke ('Henry Green', the novelist) whose 'life in the Fire Brigade sounds unendurable'.

King Zog of the Albanians, escorted by two of his bodyguards, setting out from the Ritz for one of his 'tiny, Parisian walks'.

In one night, fifteen incendiaries landed on the roof of the Ritz but were quickly put out. With its steel frame the hotel was soon regarded as a safe shelter in itself; the sixth and seventh floors were closed and as the building was so strong it was thought that any bomb damage would not percolate lower than that. During the air raids *chaise-longues* were placed in the bedroom corridors for guests to sleep on – the walls being so thick this was considered a safe place – and the basement shelter was stocked with camp beds, though some residents brought their own.

A snack bar was installed next to the Grill Room and an elaborate graffito appeared showing the Siegfried line, Hitler and a balloon-like Goering. This jape reached the ears of 'Lord Haw-Haw' who threatened that the Ritz might regret it; not long afterwards two 500 lb bombs fell near the hotel, one of them shattering the store of Baccara glass.

No. CR**1100**

City of Westminster.

Child's Respirator Fitting Card.

Name of Child *Henry Robin Russel*
(Surname first)
Address *23 Wilton Street S.W.1*
Date of Birth *Jan 21st 1940*
Date Fitted *March 4th 1940*
Where Fitted *Ritz Hotel Piccadilly*

This card to be retained by parent (or guardian) for production when distribution of Children's Respirators takes place.

P.T.O.

In spite of the bombs, the sandbags, the utility tablecloths and the ubiquitous uniforms, life at the Ritz appeared outwardly to be the same, though the shortage of such basic necessities as soap, towels and linen obviously had its effect. On 21 January 1940, for the first and only time in the seventy-five years of the Ritz's history, a baby was born in the hotel; the child's mother, Lady Howland, had wanted to be comfortable for the birth so two suites were duly fitted out at the expense of the baby boy's great-grandfather, the Duke of Bedford, husband of the 'Flying Duchess'. By a curious coincidence the baby (now the Marquess of Tavistock) is forty years later, a director of Trafalgar House. Not surprisingly, Lord

The Ritz baby's gas-mask certificate: his surname (Russell) is misspelt.

Tavistock says that he has 'always felt a particular affection and pride in the Ritz – it's very special for me.' One of his earliest memories is 'the white lampshades in the Restaurant', and he was very impressed as a child by the 'massiveness of the halls'. It is said that when he was born his first cry provoked strangers in the bar to embrace and buy one another drinks.

In the same month the hostess Emerald Cunard moved into the Ritz, having decided to close down her house in Grosvenor Square and part with some of her fine French furniture. She later went to America for a spell but returned to the Ritz with her faithful maid, Gordon, in 1942 before moving to the Dorchester.

The fall of France in the summer of 1940 led to a fresh influx of residents at the hotel and the place was soon full of refugee Royalties, aristocrats and politicians. The most celebrated of these were the Albanian Royal Family and their entourage who arrived at the hotel on 24 June 1940 after a hazardous journey by way of Greece, Turkey, Scandinavia, Holland, France, Plymouth and the Great Western Hotel, Paddington. The party consisted of King Zog, his half-American Queen Geraldine, the infant Crown Prince Leka, the King's six sisters, three nephews and two nieces, his American grandmother-in-law, plus an ADC, Chamberlain, Secretary, the Albanian *chargé d'affaires* from the Paris Embassy and the famous bodyguards. Some of the retinue stayed at the Athenaeum Court in Piccadilly but the King and Queen had a third-floor suite overlooking the park and half a dozen bodyguards were billeted in an upper floor. King Zog arrived with a mass of luggage; parts of it seemed exceptionally heavy and George, the hall porter, asked His Majesty if they contained anything of great value.

'Yes,' said King Zog, 'gold.'

The treasure was subsequently transferred from the storeroom of the Ritz to the Bank of England, where the King's secretary, Mr Martini, would withdraw a thousand-pound banknote every week.

King Zog was not happy with the hotel's air-raid shelter; he preferred something more exclusive and the Ritz accordingly converted the ladies' cloakroom for the Albanians' use as a private shelter. When a bomb landed in Piccadilly, making an enormous crater between the Berkeley and the Ritz, most of the Royal Family removed to Chelsea, but King Zog stayed put until the spring of 1941 when Lord Parmoor's house in Buckinghamshire was put at the family's disposal. Max, a waiter at the Ritz, went with the King as his butler.

Previous Ministers to Albania, like Sir Andrew Ryan and Sir Robert Hodgson, as well as friends of the country, such as General Sir Jocelyn Percy and Auberon Herbert (Evelyn Waugh's brother-in-law), came to call on King Zog at the Ritz. Queen Geraldine's lady-in-waiting, Maria Selma Zavaloni, remembers accompanying the Crown Prince (now King Leka of the Albanians) for walks in his perambulator in the park with his personal servants who could not speak English.

Mrs Christopher Sykes, the daughter of Russell Pasha, recalls the night she was sleeping next to one of the ferocious looking Albanian bodyguards in the Grill Room downstairs at the Ritz: 'It was not a very agreeable experience and I was delighted when Tommy Brand [later Viscount Hampden] offered me his bed in his room upstairs, which he had kindly vacated. However, I received some curious looks from the porter the following morning because apparently I was the third different woman to have slept there on successive nights.' Mrs Sykes says that the Ritz certainly enjoyed a tremendous vogue during the war and was, even more than ever, much used as a meeting place; at night 'it was crowded and somehow safe'. Alan Bennett set some of his brilliant allegorical play, *Forty Years On*, in the basement of the wartime Ritz.

The Aga Khan spent the war in Switzerland, but European Royalties who were seen fleetingly at the Ritz in the war included Kings George of Greece and Peter of Yugoslavia. On one moving occasion Ed Murrow, the American broadcaster, introduced Queen Wilhelmina of the Netherlands, Grand Duchess Charlotte of Luxembourg, King Haakon of Norway and King Christian of Denmark in a joint Royal transmission to the United States from the basement of the Ritz. Queen Wilhelmina, doughty symbol of the Dutch people's resistance, had tears in her eyes as she spoke into the microphone and the professional Murrow had difficulty in controlling his own emotions.

During the war years Dr Benes, the Czech President, used to entertain guests to a modest luncheon in a private room at the Ritz several times a week. Before he eventually returned to Prague, he thanked the manager, Mr Schwenter (who succeeded M. Duchene on his death in 1941), and told him that he had wished to give him a decoration for his many kindnesses; 'but soon I may be in close touch with the Russians. I am told they don't favour decorations.' Instead he gave the Swiss manager a signed photograph which remained on his desk at the Ritz until his retirement at the end of 1969.

The hotel was frequently the scene of history-making events, such as a special meeting attended by Churchill, de Gaulle and Eisenhower in the Marie Antoinette suite. When interviewed for this book, Lord Mountbatten recollected a fascinating lunch with that great commander, 'Alex' (then General Sir Harold Alexander) in 1942: 'I asked him to meet me at the Ritz because I wanted him to become my permanent Commander-in-Chief of Amphibious Operations. However, Alex said that I was a day too late for Winston had asked him to go out to Burma as GOC-in-C and he had accepted. He had, of course, told Winston that this was a difficult mission but Winston said he appreciated that and therefore, if it failed, nothing would be held against him. Nor was it. Winston kept his word and Alex didn't suffer from this setback.' Another lunchtime at the Ritz found Lord Louis, as he then was, discussing with Noel Coward a film to be based on Mountbatten's ill-fated ship HMS *Kelly*. The film was *In Which We Serve*.

Brendan Bracken relished his role as Churchill's observer and mouthpiece in London's wartime political society and the Anglo-American politician Ronald Tree, who entertained the Prime Minister at Dytchley in Oxfordshire for weekends, recalled Bracken's nocturnal activities in the hotel:

> During the winter of 1940 when I was living at the Ritz ... I would frequently be woken up at night by a banging on the door. Brendan had arrived to have a whisky and soda and talk non-stop until the mood took him to depart for his next port of call, that is to waken up some other poor unfortunate and after that, another, before finally returning to No. 10 in the early morning.

In the early years of the war food shortages were not so acute and Evelyn Waugh's diaries include references to him 'dining and lunching at the Ritz and spending a very great deal of money'. His novel *Work Suspended* includes a scene in which the narrator has fallen in love with a friend's wife. He asks the couple to luncheon at the Ritz, making up a party of six by inviting also 'a middle-aged highly reputable woman-novelist and Andrew Desart and his wife'. At the end of the lunch the narrator sees the young husband 'trying to work out why I should have spent *five pounds* [our italics] in this fashion?' The novel was published in

Dr Benes, President of Czechoslovakia and Ritz refugee, at the microphone (*top*).
Wartime view from an upper window of the Ritz (*bottom*).
Opposite General de Gaulle being interviewed at the Ritz (*top*).
Aly Khan, wayward son of the Aga, with George, the hall porter (*bottom left*).
Some have gone further than merely commenting on their likeness, believing them
to have been half-brothers.
Queen Wilhelmina of the Netherlands broadcasts to her people (*bottom right*).

1943; the previous summer a Government order had come into force limiting meals in hotels and restaurants to three courses and five shillings in price. But partly thanks to Hugh Wontner, who had already become managing director of the Savoy Group, catering establishments were permitted to charge extra for oysters and certain luxury items.

And so the voice of the mock turtle was heard in the land. Juggling with a penny's worth of meat per head and finding romantic French nomenclature for the likes of rissoles and Woolton Pie became the daily round for the chef at the Ritz, M. Avignon. He told Madame Zavaloni, with whom he discussed Crown Prince Leka's diet, that he spent sleepless nights worrying about what he could possibly find to serve up the next day. Laura Duchess of Marlborough remembers her cousin, the notoriously greedy 'Crinks' Johnstone, a junior Minister in the Government, boasting that the best meal he ever had at the Ritz was during the war; apparently he smuggled a sucking-pig, squashed amongst State papers in his despatch box, into the hotel and handed it over to the kitchens.

The Duchess of Marlborough – then married to the Earl of Dudley and a niece, incidentally, of Lady Cynthia Asquith who frequented the Ritz during the First World War – lived at the hotel for a spell after her home in Brook Street had been bombed. 'My maid used to tell me the food was terrible,' recalls the Duchess, 'but I assured her it was no better for us. Eric and I used to eat in our suite so as to avoid the inter-table jealousy in the Restaurant – "he's got more than me", etc. We wanted to put up our own pictures and so on in our suite but, unlike at Claridge's, they were never very keen on this sort of thing at the Ritz. Even though the carpets were already getting pretty worn and the taps were liable to fly off in your face, the Ritz in the war had a sense of atmosphere, a sense of occasion.'

Since all eating places cost much the same, anyone with any sympathy for the environment of the Ritz naturally headed for its beautiful Restaurant. The architectural writer James Lees-Milne, invalided out of the Irish Guards and working at the time for the National Trust, often lunched there during the war with Lady Bridget Parsons, sister of the Earl of Rosse: 'We agreed that the Ritz is no more expensive than anywhere else these days and far more agreeable.' Sometimes, though, it could become too crowded, as when Lees-Milne gave a luncheon for Lady Colefax, the interior decorator (known as 'Coalbox'), Honey Harris and Cyril Connolly. Amidst all the noise Lees-Milne 'did not hear one word Sibyl uttered, and not for one instant did she draw breath. I asked Cyril whether he had heard anything, and he said nothing at all. The party was not therefore a rollicking success as far as the host was concerned.'

At the Ritz Grill Lees-Milne and Harold Acton dined with the writer Norman Douglas, by then well into his seventies, who had come to England from Italy for the first time since 1916. Lees-Milne noted in his diary that Douglas 'hates it, and the cold of it, and the restraint, the bad food and the puritanism. Is delighted to be able to talk to the Italian waiters in the Ritz Grill in their own language.' Nancy Mitford was a frequent companion of Lees-Milne at the Ritz; once, when lunching at a table near the door of the Restaurant with Sir Robert Abdy and Lady Cunard, the latter told of how Miss Mitford's grandfather, Lord Redesdale, behaved: 'My dear, he used to accompany King Edward to Paris, where they went wenching together.' James Lees-Milne was a close friend of Nancy Mitford's brother, Tom, and they were reunited at the Ritz after Tom Mitford had been away in the Mediterranean for two and a half years: 'We went up to his suite in the Ritz – how civilized and pretty after the Dorchester and modern jazz hotels.'

The British are an adaptable, humorous race and they were at their best in the war, making fun of the shortages. When Evelyn Waugh and Nancy Mitford were lunching at the Ritz one day she indulged in a histrionic performance as to what a treat it all was. A waiter arrived at their table, bearing a covered dish which was then revealed to the accompaniment of a gushing Mitfordesque ejaculation: 'Toast!'

Dorothy Donaldson-Hudson, the campaigner for the cleaning up of Soho, had an arrangement with some cab-drivers – Ossie, Little Joe and Jenks – on the rank at Hyde Park Corner whereby she would leave the key to her flat with one of them and telephone to ask for her poodle to be brought over to the Ritz. 'Florence in the ladies' lavatory used to look after everyone's dog; she knew the owners by their dog's name.' Florence was a 'character' in the best traditions of this calling, as epitomized by Angus Wilson's 'Mrs Salad'.

Christopher Sykes's sister, the artist Angela Countess of Antrim, remembers the Ritz as a great place for 'gathering news of husbands at the wars'. The journalist and travel writer, Lord Kinross, 'was especially thoughtful, asking people for drinks before lunch whenever he came home from the Middle East and disseminating reassuring messages.'

Dame Freya Stark recollects the Ritz during the war as 'the place at whose doors one could sometimes find a taxi'. Another travel writer, Patrick Leigh Fermor, recalls how he and Xan Fielding, whose brother-in-law Lord Vivian once conducted the dance band at the Ritz, 'contrived secretly to spend a week there, draped about the rooms of a friend, who would order gargantuan breakfasts each morning ("Can't think why I've got such a ravenous appetite here, waiter") which were solemnly wheeled in while we hid in the bathroom. I think everyone knew something fishy was going on but turned a blind eye. Wartime excused much.'

Earlier in the war, when he was a guardsman in the Irish Guards, Leigh Fermor borrowed 'a boiled shirt and studs' from one of the waiters at the Ritz in order to go to a party given by the Duchess of Westminster. James Lees-Milne once described the Duchess's married life to the notorious 'Bend Or' as 'a definition of unadulterated hell'. Loelia Westminster (now Lady Lindsay of Dowhill) introduced Lees-Milne to Lady Diana Cooper at the Ritz shortly after the ageless beauty's return from the Middle East (in which setting Evelyn Waugh depicted her as 'Mrs Stitch'):

> Lady D., as she shook hands, looked at and through me with those legendary blue eyes which petrify. She does not know me and those goddess eyes were presumably assessing the strange worm which had dared rise on its tail from the mock Savonnerie carpet. Her beauty is rather divine than human. Not a line visible. Her hair, celestially golden (again mythological) all curled and thick, had, she said, just been permanently waved in Algiers by a child of nine.

Lady Diana and her son, John Julius (now Viscount Norwich), then went in to lunch with 'Chips' Channon. Thus another diarist was able to report for posterity that Lady Diana was 'looking lovelier than ever'.

Laura Duchess of Marlborough, herself a noted beauty, says that 'a lot of old queers remember the wartime Ritz with nostalgia because the Ritz bar had a special *cachet* for pick-ups.' Alastair Forbes states that 'The basement bar was once homosexual and the upstairs one hetero.' Felix Hope-Nicholson, known with his Oxford friend Roddy Lambton (Anthony Lambton, the politician's elder brother who died in 1941) as 'The Boys' at the Ritz bar, agrees that it was 'notoriously queer'. The

The basement in the blitz.

regulars there included a Colonel in charge of posting at the War Office. 'He was known as "Colonel Cutie" because he called everybody "cutie"', recalls Hope-Nicholson. 'He had an insatiable mania for meeting young 2nd Lieutenants; I was popular with him because I used to introduce lots of them.' Another character was Paddy Brodie, upon whom Evelyn Waugh partly based the character of the 'Hon. Miles Malpractice' in his novels. Brodie was apparently an alcoholic and on one occasion, when rather the worse for wear in the middle of the afternoon at the Ritz, he became convinced that he had lost a five pound note. 'He proceeded to accost the old dowagers, taking their tea in the Palm Court,' says Hope-Nicholson, 'and, when he had no luck in this direction, made the staff remove the tables and pull up the carpets in order to search for this elusive fiver. It wasn't there, of course.' Brodie's best known peccadillo was the unfortunate occasion when 'he came to the bar, having mistaken it for the *pissoir.'*

Brodie's 'special crony', says Hope-Nicholson, was Lord Holden. Other notables of the downstairs bar were Viscount Tredegar, the poet and artist, and Harold Nicolson, MP. Sir Robert Helpmann recalls: 'My friends and I used to go to the downstairs bar as it was underground and we always knew if the air-raid siren had gone as the King and Queen of Albania used to appear and sit in a back room, so we all knew that there would be a hard night's drinking until they left, which was a sign that the All Clear had gone as far as we were concerned.' Felix Hope-Nicholson remembers once falling over the sleeping Crown Prince.

In his autobiography *High Diver*, Michael Wishart, the artist,

The outrageous personality of the downstairs bar Brian Howard (left), photographed with a friend by Cecil Beaton.

describes perhaps the most remarkable character haunting the bar then, Edomie Johnson, who 'preferred to be known as Sod, an endearing diminutive of Sodomy'. Her daily routine was to rise late and drink 'all the gin she could lay her adroit hands on'. She would then go shoplifting in large department stores during the lunch hours; 'in the afternoons she rested'. Wishart writes:

> Sod's exceptional kindness endeared her to many. In the war she had become a shrine of pilgrimage to homosexuals on leave from active service. During the bombardment, the downstairs bar at the Ritz was known as 'l'Abri' (the shelter). It was here that Sod held court. She was the buggers' Vera Lynn.

Apart from Edomie Johnson, other women to be seen in the downstairs bar from time to time included Pauline Tennant, whose father ran the Gargoyle Club (haunt of Guy Burgess) and some of the daughters of the unfortunate Earl Beauchamp, who was hounded out of society by his disobliging brother-in-law, 'Bend Or' Westminster. One of the Lygon girls, 'Coot', told Felix Hope-Nicholson that once when she was staying at the Ritz in a room opposite a gluttonous Dutch businessman this person literally 'burst' and bits of him came into her room. Hope-Nicholson's sister, Marie-Jacqueline Lancaster, raised some eyebrows in 1940 by taking her friend Marie Tracy to the downstairs bar; Miss Tracy was a negress.

Mrs Lancaster is the biographer of yet another personality who frequented the downstairs bar of the Ritz, that exotic failure Brian Howard, whose outrageous behaviour is the subject of several anecdotes told about the hotel. Once some young friends of his, who were informally dressed, were detained at the door of the Ritz Restaurant; Howard insisted on knowing the reason.

'We've got Royalty, Sir', said the head waiter. 'They can't come in here dressed like that.'

'Royalty. What do you mean?' said Howard.

'King Zog, Sir.'

'King *Zog*, do you say, *King* Zog, do you mean the man who pays his bill here by chipping bits off that gold he managed to extricate from his poor country?'

Howard had a violent distaste for uniforms, and in the bar he flung a cocktail at his old friend Harold Acton, then a Flight-Lieutenant in the RAF, proclaiming sarcastically, '*à Monsieur l'Officier*'. It was the end of that friendship. When Howard was in the bar another evening, dressed in his own uniform as an Aircraftsman and deploring 'in that unmistakable and articulate voice of his ... the state of the war, the behaviour of Churchill, the equivocal outcome of the Second Front and so on', a high-ranking RAF officer sitting nearby rose to his feet and demanded the speaker's name, number and station. Breaking off his monologue for a moment, Howard said loudly over his shoulder: 'My name is Mrs Smith.'

'The trouble was,' says Felix Hope-Nicholson, 'that the Ritz bar became too chic, too popular and, above all, too queer for the authorities.' The Yorkshire landowner George Howard (no relation, it need hardly be said, to the egregious Brian; although stretching a parenthetical note to excess, *Brideshead Revisited*, in which the character of Anthony Blanche is partly based on Brian Howard, was filmed at Castle Howard) remembers that the Brigade of Guards had to put a ban on the downstairs bar. 'The War Office managed to have it shut "for repairs",' says Hope-Nicholson, 'and thus effectively closed it down.'

Robin McDouall used to stay at the Ritz during the war at 25s. a night but abandoned the practice when he 'discovered a bit of chewing gum stuck to the brass bedstead ... the American forces had arrived.' McDouall's principal memories of the Ritz in the war revolve around the legendary Mrs Keppel, Edward VII's companion whose connexion with the hotel went back to its very beginning.

Mrs Keppel arrived at the Ritz in June 1940 after escaping from Italy. Stiff-backed and immaculate, this grand old lady was a proud symbol of the Ritz in wartime. Her daughter, Violet Trefusis, described one incident, however, which reads not a little awkwardly today:

> One evening at the Ritz when bombs were raining round the hotel (one fell only a few yards away, in Green Park) an elderly Jewess burst into hysterical tears in the lounge. My mother rose, crossed over to where she was sitting, tapped her lightly on the shoulder. 'Madam', she rebuked her, 'this is not the Wailing Wall.'

McDouall says that Mrs Keppel always enjoyed first-hand intelligence about what was going on and would preface even the most humdrum remark with 'Winston [or whoever] says . . .' For example, 'Archie says I must keep my slippers by my bed so I don't tread on broken glass in case of an air raid' – 'Archie' being Sir Archibald Sinclair, Secretary of State for Air (later Viscount Thurso). She was a game old bird, always ready for anything. When McDouall discovered that the staff of the Ritz used to take their own meals at the pub opposite called The Blue Posts ('where the food was certainly much better'), he asked Mrs Keppel to try it out with him and she readily agreed. McDouall and Wyndham Goodden gave a Bohemian party at the Pheasantry, in the King's Road, in 1944, and when Mrs Keppel got wind of this she insisted on coming. Violet Trefusis was not so popular with the night porter at the Ritz after her luggage had to be retrieved from Waterloo during a doodle-bug raid. She overheard him say to his colleague: 'Well, we've 'ad V2, we've 'eard of VD, but in my opinion, V.T. is the worst of the lot!'

On 4 May 1945, 'Chips' Channon

> Had dinner with Mrs Keppel who, in spite of her years, looked magnificent. We discussed the war, and I really wondered as we talked, which war we were on to, the last war, the Boer War or the Crimean War, so eternally charming is she. I went along the corridor to the Ritz, being like everyone else, in a restless mood (all London has been on edge these last few days, waiting for the final announcement) and went on to read the latest news on the tape machine. There I read that at 9.13 a communiqué had been issued at SHAEF that the Germans had capitulated in Holland, Western Germany and Denmark, and that the cease fire will begin tomorrow at 6.0 am. We were all immensely moved, and celebrated in Kümmel, the Linlithgows especially as it means that their prisoner-of-war son, Charles . . . whom they had not seen since Dunkirk, will soon be home.

On VE Day, Channon walked

> through the Ritz which was beflagged and decorated: everyone kissed me, Mrs Keppel, the Duchess of Rutland and Violet Trefusis all seized me alternately . . . The streets were almost empty, as there is a bus-strike, and taxis refused to go out – there were a few singing people, that's all.

Marbled dignity in the lady's room, modernized during the 1930s (*top*);
and (*bottom*) the dressing table prepared for a royal visitor (note the
coin tactfully placed in the dish).
The actress Irene Worth lights up (*right*), while the present Viscount Falmouth's aunt,
Mrs Sherek (whose husband was an impresario) arranges her coiffure.

Another world war was over, and a victory bonus was distributed to the staff. The hotel had suffered considerably from 'enemy action'; in 1942, for instance, there was bomb damage on nine different occasions, plant and machinery were adversely affected, bedrooms put out of commission and the Restaurant was closed twice. Financially, all things considered, the results were at least satisfactory and savings had been made due to the restrictions on expenditure. It was simply not possible to replace things like broken china and glass, not to mention obtaining new stocks of wine, and so ironically this improved the look of the annual accounts. The chairman of the hotel, Bracewell Smith, who had succeeded James Stephens just before the war, was a no-nonsense businessman from Keighley. His start in the hotel business had come just after the First World War with the acquisition of the Shaftesbury Hotel. In the 1920s he picked up some ideas from Statler in America and opened the Park Lane Hotel in 1927, buying the Café Royal two years later. Smith entered Parliament for Dulwich in 1932 and was appropriately chairman of the Kitchen Committee of the House of Commons, running the catering department throughout the war years. His son, George (known as Guy), joined the board of the Ritz in 1941 and was promptly appointed managing director.

The bus strike referred to by Smith's fellow-MP Chips Channon in his diary entry for VE day was an augury of things to come. The austere aftermath of the war and the attitude of 'we are the masters now' seemed to hold out little hope for the Ritz. It had survived the war, enhancing its reputation in the process, but would it survive the socialist peace?

CHAPTER
VI
THE POSTWAR SCENE

The war may have been over but the privations continued; it is said that some young waiters at the Ritz were so hungry that they used to eat the cherries off the tops of the ices before serving them. During a coal strike some eighty miners, perhaps bearing in mind a Judge's famous dictum that 'justice was open to all, like the Ritz Hotel' came in and 'occupied' the Grill Room, asking for food and tea and singing 'Rock of Ages' and 'The Red Flag'. Having called them to order, Schwenter, the manager, explained that the staff were off duty and it was not possible to serve so many at such short notice. He suggested that they return the next day when he would see that they were given something to eat, free of charge; they left peacefully, shaking Schwenter by the hand and did not in fact come back, though some food was prepared for them.

In the autumn of 1946, the hotels of London were themselves engulfed in a strike which began at the Savoy where official recognition was sought for the hotel workers' union. The Ritz, which has never been unionized, had to call off lunch on 9 October, but the head waiter told the press that 'naturally we are making an exception for very important people', pointing out that Field-Marshal Viscount Alanbrooke was lunching there.

Rationing still made life difficult for the chef, M. Avignon, but by persuading many of the staff to chip in with their own sugar rations he managed to create a confectionery to carry off the prize at the first 'Hotel Olympia' after the war. Avignon did not retire until the mid-1950s – the five shilling meal limit was lifted in 1950 – and dissatisfaction with the Ritz's cuisine in the postwar years became fairly widespread. At one stage a small group of Ritz patrons calling themselves 'Friends of the Ritz' went to see Sir Bracewell Smith (who was created a baronet in 1947 following his year as Lord Mayor of London) at his suite in the Park Lane Hotel in

One of the Ritz and London's treasured postwar sights, Nubar Gulbenkian, the perennial orchid in his buttonhole, in his basketwork Rolls-Royce taxi.

order to voice their concern at the standard of the Ritz cooking, which they felt did not live up to the beautiful surroundings in which it was served. Sir Bracewell told them brusquely that he went there for his daily lunch and was quite satisfied with things; he then bade them good day.

The flamboyant man of letters Anthony Blond, whose novel *Family Business* contains a lunchtime scene at the Ritz in which the host says 'the food's all right provided you don't go for anything ambitious', remembers a splendid blow-out at the hotel that he and some Oxford friends enjoyed in the days of rationing. When they had finished the waiter asked him: 'Would you like to start all over again, Sir?'

Robert Linsley, now secretary of the Carlton Club, who worked at the Ritz for a time after the war as a *commis* waiter during his hotel training, says the kitchens were still run along classical lines: 'M. Avignon ruled the place with a rod of iron and it was very hard work.' He recalls that one waiter, who had rather come down in the world, was an alcoholic so he was mainly deployed for breakfast operations at which time there was thought to be less chance of his tippling. The veteran waiter Vincent Devivo, who has been at the Ritz for over fifty years, thinks the place has not been the same since waitresses were taken on to the staff in 1947, as, in his view, females are always unreliable.

Lord Wimborne, who used to lunch in the Restaurant virtually every day at his own special table, had died just before the war – a week, in fact, after the hotel had jogged his memory about an unpaid account of £700 – and in 1946 the neighbouring Wimborne House was offered for sale to the Ritz; an ironical twist with which to end the verbal tennis match that had taken place between the Guest family and the Ritz since the beginning of the century. For the first time since the hotel opened, the profit and loss account at the end of the 1948 financial year actually showed a profit (to the tune of just over £15,000).

The Bracewell Smiths were entitled to feel proud of their shrewd stewardship in these taxing times, but they blotted their copybook by coming up with the lamentable idea of redecorating the interior in some sort of 'modern' style. It was indeed fortunate that the invitation to prepare the new scheme was issued to a person of such taste and such high principles as Lady Colefax of Colefax & Fowler. 'To her great credit,' says James Lees-Milne, 'she turned down this tempting commission, for she was poor then. Moreover she told the management that if they engaged anyone else she would raise a clamour of opposition by getting

Pots and pans in the old kitchens (*above*); and (*below*) the Ritz chefs come out on strike, 1946.

Sir Bracewell Smith, the Ritz's chairman, visiting the Pinewood set of *London Belongs to Me* during his term of office as Lord Mayor (*top*). With him in the coach is Patricia Roc, the actress who played 'Doris Josser' in the film.
The hotel silver is cleaned downstairs (*bottom*).

her influential friends to write letters of protest to *The Times* and to raise questions in both Houses of Parliament.'

The Ritz lost its doyenne with the death of Mrs Keppel in September 1947, her widower Lieutenant-Colonel George Keppel (who had been made a Member of the Royal Victorian Order by his wife's friend Edward VII; presumably for services not rendered) only surviving her by a couple of months. While the Colonel was on his deathbed in the family suite at the Ritz, his daughter Violet Trefusis was conducting a somewhat incongruous conversation with Richard Buckle in the next room about her libretto for a ballet in which the central character was to be the Loch Ness Monster. While Buckle tried to show polite enthusiasm for this unpromising material, Mrs Trefusis went backwards and forwards from the bedroom to see whether her poor father had yet breathed his last. 'I failed to interest Freddie Ashton in the idea', Buckle recalls.

A more dramatic and tragic end befell Peter Beatty at the Ritz not long afterwards when he threw himself out of his valet's room on the sixth floor of the hotel. Younger son of the famous Admiral, Earl Beatty, and grandson of Marshall Field, the Chicago department store tycoon, Beatty had always been a highly strung person and his sight had been getting steadily worse. What particularly upset him was that he could no longer see his beloved racehorses run. Alastair Forbes remembers 'his expensive slipper lying long exposed in the kitchen area after they had carried his blind body away.'

Another much-publicized suicide at the Ritz in the postwar period was that of an erratic Frenchman, Baron Pierre de Laitre, whose activities were of some interest to international police organizations. Ironically it was with a Sussex policeman's daughter, Eileen Hill, that the playboy crook was staying at the Ritz. They posed as a married couple and it was presumed that when she made it clear to the Baron that she had no intention of marrying him, he strangled her after a violent struggle and then stuffed a silk sock – one of a pair he had recently acquired but had not paid for – down his own throat. When staff forced the locked door of the bedroom on the second floor some hours later they found two dead bodies and an empty bottle of champagne.

Lady Diana Cooper returned from Paris, where her husband had been Ambassador, the same year as the Keppels died and she and Sir Duff (as he then was) were given a celebratory dinner in the Marie Antoinette suite at the Ritz by John Sutro and Christopher Sykes. As

Lady Diana, like Oscar Wilde, hated electricity, Sykes arranged for there to be candles. About two dozen people came, including Oggie Lynn (once described by Elizabeth Bibesco in Charles de Noailles's sitting room at the Ritz as 'a traveller in liaisons'), Lady Cunard (attending possibly her last function of this sort), and Evelyn Waugh and his wife, the former Laura Herbert. John Sutro recalls that Waugh 'capriciously changed the cards, vexed that he was not sitting next to Diana Cooper'.

The Waughs would often eat at the Ritz in the postwar period: a typical diary entry tells us that 'Laura and I went to London on Thursday and had our hair cut and ate caviar, grouse and peaches at the Ritz, to cheer ourselves up.' Sometimes a shorthand 'Good Ritz' is employed in the diary. Among Evelyn Waugh's companions at the Ritz in these years were Lady Diana Cooper; Nancy Mitford; Lady 'Maimie' Lygon (then still married to Prince Vsevolode of Russia and daughter of the Lord Beauchamp who Waugh may have drawn on for the character of 'Lord Marchmain' in *Brideshead Revisited*) with whom he 'got drunk' one day when he had come up to London after his 'disgust' with his family 'grew past bearing'; Lady Pamela Berry (now Lady Hartwell); Angela Laycock (daughter of the Duke of Windsor's old friend Freda Dudley Ward); and the present Earl and Countess of Longford. The fare was usually to Waugh's liking ('Lobster Newburg and Tournedos Rossini. Excellent'). When dining at the Ritz beside Caroline Blackwood, the novelist (then married to Lucian Freud), before a 'Roman party' he ascribed his nausea to the fact that he 'imprudently drank two bottles of Vichy water before starting'; he 'had to leave the table and be sick.' He also regretted drinking some 'spurious chartreuse' after a 'good dinner' of 'Caviare, crème Germiny, Tournedos Rossini, pears, white and red Burgundy' (the bill, in 1955, was £10) with Ann Fleming, wife of the creator of James Bond. The Restaurant, however, was 'almost empty'. In the same autumn, at the time Waugh was about to reply to Nancy Mitford's original 'Noblesse Oblige' article in *Encounter*, he was sitting with Mrs Fleming when a man 'whose name I did not know' came up to them.

'I am sorry you didn't put anything about Lady L. into your novel', he said.

'I barely knew her', Waugh replied.

'She was my mistress for three years.'

After Sir Max Beerbohm's 'ill-attended' funeral at St Paul's, Waugh lunched ('raw steak') at the Ritz with Osbert Lancaster and noticed Teresa

Jungman in the Restaurant with Viscount Margesson. One Sunday at Mass he 'met the shambling, unshaven and as it happened quite penniless figure' of Graham Greene (Greene had 'emptied his pockets into the box for African missions') and took him to the Ritz for a cocktail, giving him sixpence with which to tip the porter who looked after his hat. Towards the end of his life Waugh noted in his diary:

> I must have given my hat many hundreds of times to the old porter at the Ritz . . . The other day when I came to leave after luncheon he was not on duty, so I went behind his counter and collected my belongings. In my hat he had put a label with the word 'Florid'.

Schwenter, the manager, on the other hand addressed all the guests by name and kept a permanent record of their likes and dislikes. 'We file the names and address of the client, the type of accommodation he likes and any other fads he has', said Schwenter in 1969 (the year he finally retired). The ratio of staff to guest used to be three to one before Selective Employment Tax; since then it has ideally, though not always practically, been two to one.

That larger than life Ritz figure, Nubar Gulbenkian, who had a permanent suite at the hotel, always, according to Schwenter, 'wanted things out of season and no matter where they came from – Spain, Italy – they had to be flown in specially. In the grouse season he had to have grouse by the evening of the Twelfth. He wouldn't wait until the 13th.' Gulbenkian's father, 'Mr Five Per Cent', died alone in his hotel bedroom at Lisbon in 1955. Father and son were very different – Calouste was a paranoid recluse, Nubar an expansive extrovert – and had fallen out over a trifling expense account bill for a meal which Nubar had submitted before the last war. The day his father died, however, Nubar changed his beige Rolls-Royce for a black one. Later he took to being driven around London in a special taxi with a Rolls-Royce engine and basketwork body; this was more suitable for metropolitan traffic as, according to Gulbenkian, it could 'turn on a sixpence – whatever that is'. When asked to describe his 'present position' on a form, he wrote 'enviable' and he always made great play of being very rich indeed, but in fact he was not as wealthy as everyone thought. He was a generous man though, and is said to have tipped the liftman at the Ritz handsomely on every journey, up and down.

Evelyn Waugh, a notable feeder at the Ritz, photographed by his old private-school victim Cecil Beaton at home, or rather not 'at home'.

Murder at the Ritz: Eileen Hill, the policeman's daughter who died at the hands of the French Baron.

Lady Diana Cooper, the ageless beauty and now the *doyenne* of the Ritz.

Schwenter, the manager, does his homework in *Who's Who*.

View across Green Park (*above*), embracing Buckingham Palace, from a Ritz window.
Nubar Gulbenkian's valet, Jim d'Almeido, attends to his master's evening shirting (*right*).

As honorary Commercial Counsellor for Iran in London, he undertook the Embassy's entertaining programme at the Ritz (where the Shah himself has often stayed) and once gave a particularly lavish party for General de Gaulle in this capacity. At one dinner he had to instruct the Canadian Roy Thomson, the future Press baron, how to eat quails' eggs; Thomson was peering quizzically at the shells. Although Gulbenkian moved round the corner to a flat in Arlington House, above the once fashionable Caprice restaurant, some years before he died in 1972, it was at the Ritz that his widow gave a party in 1973 in his memory. Marie Gulbenkian told the guests (all of whom had attended his memorial service the year before) that this was 'Nubar's party, not mine'.

The British aristocracy, for whom the 1950s was a surprisingly prosperous decade confounding the gloomy prognostications of the age of austerity after the war, continued to patronize the Ritz in some force.

George Howard, who stayed there a lot at this time despite finding the service rather slow on the bedroom floors, had the disconcerting experience of coming across his 'double' at the Ritz – a generously built Welsh actor known as 'The Voice', who was then a popular villain in the new television series *Garry Halliday* (with Terence Longdon). Although he says it was never one of his haunts, the Marquess of Linlithgow – whose forthcoming release from Germany was toasted in Kümmel by his parents, Chips Channon and others in 1945 – remembers getting 'lost in a London "pea soup" with my wife and two guests and begged the Ritz for a room – fortunately, we were theatre-dressed at the time. They gave us a suite for the night; it turned out to be Lord Rosebery's – I hope he never knew. They had the honesty not to make a charge.'

Lord Rosebery's friendly rival on the turf, Lord Carnarvon, who had divorced his second wife Tillie Losch after the war, gave a dinner for sixty people in the Marie Antoinette suite on the engagement of his son Lord Porchester (now The Queen's racing manager) to Jean Wallop from Big Horn, Wyoming. 'I asked all Porchester's old girl friends', recalls the sporting peer. The Aga Khan, that other Ritz veteran, was still very much in evidence, occupying the whole floor with his one-hundred-strong entourage and private chef. On Derby night the Ritz was decorated with brown carnations grown to match the Aga's racing colours. The Aga's charming, if wayward son, Aly, whose life epitomized the old jest about fast women and slow horses, was a very close friend of Lord Carnarvon. One morning they were having breakfast together in Aly's sitting room at the Ritz and Aly confided in Lord Carnarvon about his intimate problems: although barely middle-aged the Prince was suffering from prostate trouble ('the old man's disease') which he felt had been brought on by the ministrations of a gentleman in Cairo who specialized in the prolonging of sexual pleasure, a facility of which Aly Khan had taken somewhat excessive advantage. The worldly Earl was able to recommend a revolutionary new electric treatment pioneered by an American surgeon; Aly Khan, who was on his way to Paris, expressed his gratitude for the tip which he said he would follow up.

That night Lord Carnarvon was playing bridge at the Portland Club and did not return to the Ritz until about midnight. When he arrived at the hotel he was surprised to see George, the hall porter, still on duty. 'George asked me solicitously if I'd like some whisky or brandy', recalls Lord Carnarvon, 'and took me into his little room. He told me that I must

The Aga Khan leads in *Masaka* (W. Nevett up) after beating King George VI's *Angelola* in the Oaks, 1948.

The Earl of Carnarvon, for whom the Ritz has been his London home since 1924, studies form in the hall with his son, Lord Porchester (*top*); and (*bottom*) Aly Khan and Rita Hayworth set out for Ascot after the police had dispersed the crowds outside the Ritz, 1949.

prepare myself for some bad news; I thought it must be one of my children and braced myself for the shock. He then said: "Our dear friend Aly was in a bad motor smash today in Paris and his neck was broken." He had died through his neck snapping as the seat belt held him in.'

George was as one of the Aga Khan's family; the Aga called him 'Honourable' and he handled all manner of business for both him and Aly, apart from the placing of bets. One of Peter Quennell's abiding memories of the Ritz is seeing 'Aly Khan seated cross-legged, like some extraordinary Oriental gnome, on the Greek hall porter's desk telephoning to his bookmaker.' George got his job at the Ritz on the strength of a recommendation from his compatriot Sir Basil Zaharoff, the Armaments magnate, and worked there for 48 years. His reminiscences were published in 1959; the copy of the book consulted in connexion with the research for this work is stamped 'Etobicoke Public Library: *Discard*' which is a slightly unkind verdict on *George of the Ritz*. This great Ritz character finally retired in 1961 aged 77, and within a month he was dead. Although he had handled millions of pounds in his time he left only £417 in his will and his widow put this down to the fact that he was 'a Greek'. 'All Greeks', she said, 'are born gamblers. He picked too many losers.'

The landowner Henry de Vere Clifton was one of George's benefactors; he once gave him a plot of land at Lytham, in Lancashire. The son of that extraordinary figure Violet Clifton, who wrote a prize-winning biography of her explorer husband called *The Book of Talbot* and ended her life as a nun, this even more eccentric poetaster retained permanent suites at both the Ritz and the Dorchester. When asked why he felt the latter to be necessary by George's successor, Victor Legg, de Vere Clifton answered: 'If I'm passing down Park Lane and feel tired, then I've got somewhere to go to.' One evening in the middle of the rush hour, de Vere Clifton telephoned down to Victor and asked him for a limousine to take him down to Brighton there and then. Before setting off with the chauffeur he demanded an old lemonade bottle of Victor (who imagined the old boy was 'incontinent or something'). When they arrived at the sea front in Brighton, the chauffeur was instructed to go down to the water's edge and fill up the bottle; they then doubled back to London and the Ritz, where de Vere Clifton repaired to his suite clutching the object of his mission. Later that night he came downstairs and accosted Victor with an air of much satisfaction. 'I've just had a nice refreshing bath,' he said, 'a real sea-water bath.'

'Every time you open your mouth,' said Tallulah Bankhead to George, 'everybody expects you to be polite and every time I open mine they expect me to be funny. Which is harder?' George, however, when sorely provoked, was not always polite. The Duke of Marlborough who described the scene at the Ritz in 1918 to his future wife Gladys Deacon (later to have him watched coming in and out of the hotel by private detectives), once called George 'a bloody foreigner'.

'And I'm proud to be one,' the Cretan replied.

'Why?' barked the Duke.

'I don't want to be English if it means being as rude as you are,' said George.

Tallulah Bankhead returned to the Ritz several times after the war, staying there during her rather less than successful cabaret season at the ailing Café de Paris. When filming *Fanatic* over here in the 1960s she slipped and fell down the steps of the hotel on the day she arrived.

The richest man in the world, Paul Getty, lived in a suite in the Ritz after the war. His lady friend had to make do with the old courier's room, which did not have its own bath; when they moved to the Duke of Sutherland's old seat, Sutton Place, she took to telephoning her mother every week so the multi-billionaire installed a coin box. 'Of course he was notoriously mean', recalls Lady Diana Cooper. 'When I was lunching with him at the Ritz once, I had to make a telephone call so I went and did so at the entrance to the Restaurant and told the man there to put it on Mr Getty's bill — it was only a local call — but I was told that Mr Getty wouldn't like this as he checked his bills very thoroughly.' The door of Lady Diana's house in Little Venice, Paddington, bears the legend on the knocker: 'The gift of J. Paul Getty'. She explains: 'I used to rag him all the time about how I needed a proper front door and wouldn't it be nice if he could give me one; well, he finally did and I had this inscription put on it as a joke. When I told him, straight-faced, about this, he was quite overcome with emotion.' A famous photograph of Getty was taken outside the Ritz by a *Time-Life* photographer who had arranged for a barrowboy to lie in wait for the billionaire with a large brown paper bag full of pennies. When Getty emerged from the Ritz, the barrowboy, on instructions, poured the coppers on to the pavement; in a reflex action, Getty was on his knees and snap went the camera shutter.

Someone else rich through oil but much more open-handed who also used to live at the Ritz was the Shell heiress Olga Deterding. She loved the hotel, which was her favourite, but in 1956 she temporarily abandoned the high life and went to work in Dr Albert Schweitzer's leper colony in French Equatorial Africa. 'Having so much money makes it necessary for me to cleanse myself', said Miss Deterding. As her close friend Alan Whicker (to whom the Ritz 'has always been just a passing pub') says, Olga Deterding 'had a marvellous sense of humour' and he tells a story that endeared her to him enormously: 'She was living at the Ritz with her lover. He decided to leave but she didn't want him to go – so she threw his trousers out of the window.'

On St Valentine's Day 1957 another rich young lady who was to cast aside sybaritic values and go 'up the junction', Nell Dunn, married Jeremy Sandford (later to become famous for his moving television play *Cathy Come Home*) and the reception was held at the Ritz. Sandford, son of the founder of the Golden Cockerel Press, wanted to leave the reception by way of a balloon from Green Park but was unable to get the necessary permission. Augustus John, then nearly 80, came up from Fordingbridge for the party dressed in his most casual clothes.

This informality at the Ritz caused a mild sensation, but Anthony Blond claims that he never had any trouble going into the Ritz without a tie in the 1950s. Even before that, when he was at Oxford, he remembers a notably scruffy undergraduate (unusual in those days) who wanted to cash a cheque at the Ritz. The staff agreed and he asked them:

'How can you be sure I'm all right?'

'*We* know, sir, we know,' was the reply.

Blond's friend Nancy Spain, the journalist, used to judge the quality of an hotel or a restaurant by whether it objected to her habitual trouserings; the Savoy apparently did object but Claridge's and the Ritz did not.

A lady with an even deeper voice than Miss Spain, Fenella Fielding, the actress, sang a duet in her native tongue, Roumanian, with Princess Calimaki, a familiar figure in the hotel for many years, at a riotous Ritz lunch given for the cast of Sandy Wilson's musical of Firbank's *Valmouth*, which transferred from the now restored Lyric Theatre, Hammersmith, to the now defunct Savile in 1959.

The journalist Ian Dunlop reminisces about the Ritz in the late 1950s with nostalgic affection: 'The gents was the best lavatory in Great Britain; the attendant was somebody pleased to see you and you were pleased to see him. He'd say: "Here, you'd better do something about that dandruff, sir" and I'd say: "Joe, what do I back next week, I haven't backed

In a theatrically 'Twenties' gesture the ageing Tallulah Bankhead sips champagne from a slipper during a 1950s press conference at the Ritz.

a winner for months – you're on a fiver if it wins". He'd tell me to "Try this one" and they were quite good a lot of the time.

'I loved the Edwardian baroque, the glamorous Palm Court, the water dribbling down the lady in the nude.' Sometimes Dunlop would stay there: 'You'd get a very tiny room which up to the end of the 1950s was about fifty bob a night; even a suite was about 25 quid. The small rooms were dirt cheap, much cheaper than you could get in the Earls Court. The Ritz looked that grand; it *was* that grand; nobody knew it was that cheap, see?

'The Ritz was always the cheapest place to go to and, if you wanted

Olga Deterding, the Shell heiress who threw her lover's trousers out of a Ritz window.

'Laurie's bar': Laurie Ross in the centre.

A characteristically cheerful expression on the face of J. Paul Getty, the less than generous multi-billionaire who lived in a suite at the Ritz after the Second World War (*left*). Nell Dunn and Jeremy Sandford (then described as a 'surrealist writer') leave the Ritz after their wedding reception, St Valentine's Day 1957 (*far left*).

to calculate the value, it was always the best value to go to. One went there to see people one liked and knew. Some people were very rich; some people were very glamorous in the gossip column manner but most of them knew each other and liked each other – that was the point. It was rather seedy which kept a lot of people you didn't like out of it and also the Edwardian baroque kept a lot of people away; then the bad food kept a lot of people away too.'

Dunlop recalls that the career of John Aspinall, the gambling club proprietor and friend of the vanished Earl of Lucan, was launched at the Ritz. 'He took a suite there and played poker with lots of rich young men and didn't do very well; he lost quite a lot of money. At one point he found himself with nowhere to go and an enormous bill to pay, so he borrowed from the only millionaire he knew who used the Ritz, Gerry Albertini, and with that money he bought his way out of the place and started the then illegal *chemin de fer* craze . . . This led to a change in the law which allowed people to gamble. He made losing immense sums of money respectable amongst respectable people.'

Dunlop once raised the *maître d'hôtel*'s blood pressure by offering him luncheon vouchers in the Restaurant. 'The Rivoli Bar, upstairs, was a place where hardly anybody knew you very much,' says the journalist, 'and you could go and have a drink with the person you shouldn't be having a drink with. If you wanted to see people whom you knew you went downstairs to the basement bar where Laurie held court and everybody knew everybody.'

Graham Greene and Max Reinhardt, the publisher, who was a friend of César Ritz's son Charles, were but two of the regulars at the popular 'Laurie's bar', as it came to be known. One of Laurie Ross's most faithful customers, Major Donald Lindsay, followed him from the Carlton where he was a barman in the 1920s (and where, incidentally, Ho-Chi-Minh was a pastry cook) and left him £300 in his will. 'He never changed,' said Laurie of the Major, 'that type didn't. His favourite drink was gin and tonic, but he would always have the odd martini. I used to talk to him quite a bit. He liked to speak of his memories and always had a good word to say about the hundreds of people he knew. He took two or three gins before dinner but he was the kind who had learnt to hold his drink.' Sometimes Laurie had to deal with those who could not; a young publisher and his secretary were being pestered by a drunk a few years before the bar closed on Laurie's retirement in 1976 and when they nervously ignored the old soak's invitation to join him in yet another cocktail he proceeded to blow a revolting raspberry at the couple. Seeing that matters were verging on the personal, Laurie intervened: 'Not in the Ritz Bar, sir, please', he admonished. '*Not* in the Ritz Bar.'

Otto von Arx, the night porter, did not have a chance to say anything just after midnight on 26 January 1959 when, as he described it, 'a young man dashed through the swing doors, dumped this big fox on the carpet and ran out . . .' The fox, a fine specimen with a white-tipped brush, was dead. 'In all my 41 years here,' said von Arx (known as 'John'), 'I've never seen anything like it.'

Exactly the same phrase was on the lips of Jock Macleod, the carriage attendant or 'linkman' at the Ritz for forty years (until he retired in 1974), after an ugly scene outside the hotel the following summer. The Prime Minister of the Congo, Lumumba, was staying in the hotel and before his departure gave dinner in the Restaurant to Sir Edward Adjaye, the Ghanaian High Commissioner in London. Events in the Congo were the cause of some concern at that time and there was a demonstration of Mosleyites parading outside the Ritz with banners bearing the legend 'RAPERS OF CHILDREN – GO HOME' and shouting that 'the dirty black swine' should go back where they had come from, and other epithets. Sir Edward came down the steps of the Ritz into Arlington Street and was making for his car when a man leapt from the crowd and struck him repeatedly; the High Commissioner (who had possibly been mistaken for Lumumba) was thrown back against his car before being knocked to the ground where a woman started to kick him. Ex-Guardsman Macleod then gallantly intervened to save Sir Edward from further punishment.

Times were a-changing and in 1961 Marie-Louise Ritz, César's widow, who had last been seen at the London hotel for the Queen's Coronation in 1953, died in Paris aged 94. What would she have made of the so-called 'Swinging Sixties'? A motley crew of slick operators in the rag trade, showbiz and property-dealing was named the 'new classless aristocracy' by the gossip columnists and, though it took little more than a decade for many of these trendy 'young meteors' to burn themselves out, one cannot underestimate the effect of the Beatle Age on British society. The real aristocracy began to take its cue from this 'aristocracy' of a new and bogus kind. Traditional aristocratic values were abandoned by the would-be fashionable who aped the fashion and manners of the proletariat. To the chroniclers of London life the only aristocrats worth a mention were those who had been accepted by the new swinging élite. The social revolution for so long predicted had come about, but not quite in the way the sociologists had imagined; it was materialism and neophilia running riot.

The morality, or lack of it, of the 'Nineteen-Sexies' is brilliantly captured in an excruciatingly dated article called 'Doing it in Style' by Donald Wiedenman in the old *Queen*, which advised the reader on how to spend a dirty weekend in London:

> Without doubt, there is only one hotel to stay in for a really old-fashioned, slightly camp Proper Affaire, and that is the Ritz. Amidst mirrors, gilt and fading elegance, the Ritz offers the best service, the most discreet staff, the biggest bath tubs, and the most intriguing atmosphere – you can still actually meet behind the aspidistra . . . The Gentleman, if he has been to the Ritz before, must use the same name he used the last time, as the staff have particularly good memories in this department. They will, however, turn a blind eye to the fact that you are not with the same Lady . . .
> There are, alas, very few double beds at the Ritz.

The couple are then recommended to go to Jules Bar for vodka martinis (watch out for William Hickey); lunch at Wheelers; copulate back at the Ritz (having drawn the curtains and lit the incense); bathe together with tumblers of champagne (playing 'Bubble Boats' with the tumblers); return to bed; take champagne cocktails in the Rivoli Bar downstairs; go to *Hair* (fondling each other during nude scene; more champagne in the interval and then dancing with their friends in the cast on stage at the end); dine (caviar and Châteaubriand) and dance at Annabel's (the 'disc dolly's' name is provided in the text) to *Un Homme et Une Femme*; back to the Ritz by the hired Rolls; bed (and more incense); bathe together in the morning (after oysters and champagne); return to bed; go shopping in Bond Street (Gucci and Michael Fish, 'long a good friend') and Kensington Antique Market (unisex pink velvet trouser suit); drink milkshakes at Yankee Doodle; stock up with pornography in Soho; back to the Ritz; smoke marijuana in the bedroom; another bath together (while the Lady reads the heavily illustrated *Ups and Downs of a Boy Named Paul*); more

The Rolling Stones (as they were, with Brian Jones on the right) just outside their favoured hotel in Green Park.

copulation; dinner at the Golden Duck in Hollywood Road (the Lady wearing see-through kaftan, the Gentleman leather trousers and a suede waistcoat); mini-cab back to the Ritz; brunch next morning at the Café Royal (reading Jilly Cooper, a friend of the Gentleman's, out loud – it's Sunday); walk in park; organize pot party in bedroom at Ritz (curtains drawn, candles lit, incense burning); mixed bathing encouraged; fish and chips sent out for; vigorous copulation; out gambling at the Pair of Shoes; walk back to the Ritz ('now as friendly as home'); bed (finish incense); check bruises in morning (nightdress from Fortnum's to shield these from husband) . . . savour 'Meaningful Memories'.

A mood statement indeed. However, as Ian Dunlop pointed out, not everybody likes the Ritz. Anthony Blond gave a launching party (a flop) for the raunchy novel *The Carpetbaggers* by Harold Robbins who was staying there; he hated the place and swiftly decamped to the Oliver Messel Suite at the Dorchester. Cilla Black told the gossip columnist of the *Sun* who took her to tea at the Ritz that it was 'not very fab'. Twiggy was more sympathetic to the atmosphere, and the now middle-aged Rolling Stones have been faithful clients over the years. David Bailey, the photographer, made a television film of Sir Cecil Beaton at the Ritz and persuaded him to sing a duet of 'If You Were the Only Girl in the World' with his old private-school chum Cyril Connolly in the Palm Court. Andy Warhol (still a Ritz regular) and his entourage took a suite when they

Andy Warhol: still a Ritz regular.

were launching one of their films; Richard Buckle went along to interview the pop artist and Paul Morrissey, the director. 'Andy Warhol was delighted with the euphony of my name and kept on repeating "dickybuckle,",' as if it was one word', recalls the ballet critic (whose own contribution to the Swinging Sixties was to describe Lennon and McCartney as the greatest composers since Schubert). 'The interview was an extraordinary affair; my photographer, Henry Pembroke, took shots of Joe d'Alessandro, the Star of the film, in the nude sitting on the loo.'

Buckle's publisher, Lord Weidenfeld, is a modern institution at the Ritz; one of the porters has never forgotten his surprise at seeing the bulky figure skip across Piccadilly on his way to lunch – 'like a large gazelle'. The Ritz is a favourite place of his for giving parties and commissioning books; 'few of them ever written, I may say', adds Quentin Crewe, who sees the Ritz's clientele as 'an interesting mixture of the horsy, the smart and the decadent'. The Director of the Victoria and Albert Museum Dr Roy Strong's memories of the Ritz include 'being lured by Lord Weidenfeld into writing some book or other', as well as tea with Duncan Grant, the artist, and 'lunches given by people of the ilk of Jackie Kennedy in the marvellous dining room'.

Dr Strong's former colleague at the museum, the art and architectural historian, the Knight of Glin, and his second wife, the former Olda Willes, had their wedding reception at the Ritz in 1970: a quintessential gathering of the smart and fashionable. The highlight was when 'Knightie' danced an Irish jig with the photographer Lord Rossmore (briefly engaged to Marianne Faithfull) and Garech Browne, the patron of the Chieftains and brother of the ill-fated Tara Browne whose death in a motor smash was the inspiration for the Beatles' song, 'A Day in the Life'.

Table No. 29 in the Restaurant would often hold Jeremy Thorpe, who loves the Ritz. 'I invited my first mother-in-law there to meet her for the first time over lunch,' he says, 'and proposed to my second wife there – also at lunch.' It was at lunch too, of course, that Thorpe saw Peter Bessell, MP; a meal of which much was made by the prosecution at the Old Bailey during 'the trial of the century'.

Edward Heath also likes Table 29, where he has been seen tucking into his favourite food – oysters and partridges. It has been noticed that Sir Harold Wilson finds it restful to remove his shoes under the table when eating at the Ritz. Another former Prime Minister and more frequent client of the Ritz, Harold Macmillan, was somewhat alarmed in the summer of 1972 by shrieks from ladies eating nearby until he spotted a field mouse which had come in from the park through the open French windows. An excitable Spanish waiter wanted to shoot it but the Restaurant manager, Marcel Hoeffler, said 'we have all become very fond of it and like to think of it as our mascot.'

The early 1970s had worse threats to the Ritz's calm than field mice; IRA bomb scares became a regular hazard. On 9 October 1975 a bomb exploded at 9 o'clock in the evening by Green Park underground station; it blew the bus shelter towards the nearby Ritz and one man in the queue was killed and eighteen others hurt. Before that terrible incident, however, the Restaurant was only cleared twice because of bomb threats; most of those received were hoaxes. A dealer in rare books from Chicago, who has been coming to the Ritz with his family for some twenty years, remembers one bomb scare in the early 1970s when he and his wife had just arrived at the hotel from Venice. 'I'd just drawn a bath,' he says, 'when an emergency notice came round saying that we had to evacuate the hotel as quickly as possible as a bomb was expected to go off ... so everyone had to file out – as they were, ladies in their *peignoirs* and that sort of thing – and we all congregated on the other side of Piccadilly, looking and feeling rather foolish. Of course it was a bad place to be as we'd have got the full blast of the shrapnel. In the end we all trooped off to the 'Blue Posts' pub where we had a jolly party until the "all clear".'

Ten years or so before the London bombings some people were worried that the Ritz's structure might voluntarily be dismantled by the Bracewell Smith ownership. Ever since the plan to redecorate the interior unsympathetically after the war, it had clearly been essential to have the Ritz listed as a building of architectural merit and historic interest so as to protect it from such risks in the future. But however important it may be architecturally (Sir Hugh Casson has called it 'a distinguished Edwardian pioneer' and Peter Wilson, of Sotheby's, 'the prototype of a style of architecture that can never be revived') it is unlikely to appeal to a socialist government. The 'listing' of the Ritz was not in fact proposed by the advisory committee of the Ministry of Housing until 1960; in the committee's view the Ritz was 'one of the best buildings of its day'. At just about the time the first Wilson administration assumed office, however, the recommendation – which had just been sat upon meanwhile, in the usual bureaucratic manner – was overruled; listing was apparently thought to be 'inexpedient'. A spokesman for the Ministry told the

Victorian Society that 'having regard to the particular function of the building, it will not be listed.' Nicholas Ridley, MP (a great-nephew of Sir Jasper Ridley who used to dine with Lady Cynthia Asquith at the Ritz in the First World War) raised the matter in the Commons a few weeks after the octogenarian Sir Bracewell Smith, still in the chair, was quoted in the press as saying:

> We are free to develop it, if possible. We would be the developers, but redevelopment is out of mind at the moment. It is a very attractive building, but it is not economical. We would have to pull it down to construct a modern hotel. A lot of space is wasted. To bring it up to modern standards, one cannot adapt it. We would want to retain the outline.

Richard Crossman, to his eternal credit, exercised his authority as the Minister for Housing and personally saw to it that the Ritz was 'listed'; conservationists heaved a sigh of relief. Peter Fleetwood-Hesketh wrote in the *Daily Telegraph*:

> The Ritz is not only a building of very high architectural quality. It is an institution, as much of London as St Paul's Cathedral or the Houses of Parliament. To the many who have known and loved it all their lives, it is the centre of London and therefore, of the world.

It had also been the centre of endless speculation about take-over bids since the Ritz Hotel (London) Ltd had become a public company in 1952 with shares readily available on the open market: in 1954 the name of Stavros Niarchos was bruited abroad; and after Sir Bracewell's death in January 1966 the rumours intensified – Maxwell Joseph said that he would be 'interested in doing a deal' for the Ritz Hotel. Sir Bracewell was succeeded in the baronetcy and chairmanship by his son, George ('Guy'), who had the exterior of the hotel cleaned in 1967 at a cost of £10,000. In 1972, Sir Charles Clore (who had held 25 per cent of the stock for some years) joined the board and the rumours then attached to him, before switching to the financier James Goldsmith.

The annual general meetings of these years had their moments of acrimony, though the stormiest scene, in 1969 – when a proposal by Sir Alexander Korda's son that Queen Frederika should be given free accommodation at the hotel was booed to the echo – had nothing to do with the shares. Finally, at the AGM of 5 April 1976, Sir Guy Bracewell Smith was able to tell the shareholders that the hotel was being taken over by the Trafalgar House group. The chairman had a fairly rough ride from some disgruntled shareholders who felt that Trafalgar had got it on the cheap, which they had, but Sir Guy calmed them down and was thanked for his patience. He replied, referring to his experience in the chair at Highbury, that 'It is not as bad as the Arsenal.'

Another era had ended at the Ritz. Its panegyric was given by Peregrine Worsthorne, who defined the charm of the postwar Ritz as 'precisely that it was not all Ritzy, in the sense of being conspicuously luxurious ... the glitter had long since faded and shabbiness set in. The place was usually empty, kept alive by memories of former glories and a clientele who preferred nostalgia to comfort.' Worsthorne went on to say that 'ever since I can remember, the Ritz has been going downhill'.

It was by no means unusual in the 1960s for example to see a mouse scuttling across the slightly threadbare carpets of the Palm Court. And the food was sometimes second-rate.

But for me these defects were the source of its charm, since they kept away all but the dedicated devotees. So there was never any difficulty in getting a table or a room, and the staff was always pleased to welcome one like a long-lost friend. Indeed it often seemed as if one had the whole place to oneself ... Peace and quiet always reigned, as in a museum.

Needless to say, the place was losing money hand over fist. The owners made no effort to keep up with the times. Modern conveniences, like dial telephones in the bedrooms were frowned on as newfangled gadgets, fit only for commercial travellers. So businessmen went elsewhere as did everyone accustomed to modern living ...

... 'in' people today spell prices that I cannot afford, people whom I cannot tolerate and, sooner rather than later, an atmosphere which will bear no relation at all to the Ritz I came to love ... It was unique because it was the only grand hotel in London which was never crowded, never noisy – a refuge into which one crept to feed, not on oysters and champagne, but on memories of a past world.

Ernest Bishop takes a table reservation at the door of the Restaurant.

For Worsthorne the postwar Ritz had come to mean 'a certain elegiac style which only lack of money could preserve.'

Schwenter, the manager since the early years of the war, had been succeeded by Geoffrey Grahame, a sometime regimental Sergeant-Major in the Grenadier Guards, who started in the hotel business as a *commis* waiter at the Savoy, worked at the May Fair Hotel and then at the Bracewell Smiths' Park Lane where he was deputy manager for ten years.

Perhaps the best known figure of all at the Ritz, Bishop, decided to retire at the time of the takeover. Ernest Bishop had joined the Ritz as a page boy in January 1924 and was the first member of the staff to achieve fifty years' service in the hotel. He told the writer Denis Hart, who wrote a profile of this much-loved figure in the *Telegraph Magazine*, that Schmid, the original hall porter, used to beat him with a stick but he found his *métier* taking table bookings for the Restaurant on the telephone and ended up as 'Restaurant receptionist'. Hart describes his 'apotheosis' as when the Countess of Rosse once presented him to The Queen Mother in these terms: 'This, Ma'am, is Bishop, dear friend of the family.'

Peter Quennell describes Bishop as 'about five feet tall with a very high collar and an extremely smart uniform who was the emissary, and now and then, I suppose, the Leporello, of all the hotel's most dissipated clients – among others Ed Stanley [the late Lord Stanley of Alderley], who once told me that when he was lunching with a woman friend and had forgotten to send her a promised bouquet the day before, he summoned Bishop and upbraided him for having failed to execute his order; at which Bishop, immediately grasping the situation, begged them both to accept his deep apologies – he had been extremely busy yesterday; and the commission had somehow slipped his mind ...'

In fact Bishop had, as the Marchese Mattei says, 'the most extraordinary memory for people, knew everyone.' Denis Hart was shown Bishop's autograph book; the first entry is for the singer Galli-Curci and as he turned the pages names such as John Barrymore, John Count McCormack, Marie Dressler, Elinor Glyn, Tallulah Bankhead ('Can I sign on the same page as Tallulah and still be pure', asked Peggy O'Neal), Hermione Baddeley (who signed under General de Gaulle, murmuring as she did so 'I've always wanted to be underneath a big man') and Bernard Shaw cropped up. Shaw initially refused to sign, saying 'Oh no, I'm sorry I don't sign autographs', but Lady Astor interjected: 'This is one time when you will, because this is for my little friend.'

CHAPTER
VII

TRAFALGAR TAKE OVER

At the beginning of 1975, the year before Trafalgar House took over the Ritz, the group's young chairman, Nigel Broackes, was having one of his fairly regular lunches there when he found a pearl in one of the oysters he was eating. This was an unusual discovery in an English mollusc and Marcel Hoeffler, the Restaurant manager, duly placed the pearl in a small envelope which he inscribed 'Pearl at the Ritz. 14.1.75'. For Broackes, who describes himself as 'a faintly superstitious person', this event helped reinforce his morale at a time when few businessmen were taking a particularly optimistic view of the economy.

Broackes's own connexion with the Ritz had already extended beyond lunching there over the years. When he was an estate agent he had tried to buy the hotel for a lady named Mrs Amy Rose, who had backing from Maxwell Joseph of the Grand Metropolitan group, in 1958. By an interesting coincidence Broackes's father, a solicitor, had been concerned with setting up the company of the Park Lane Hotel, the Bracewell Smiths' other principal establishment.

In March 1975 Broackes received a visit from the Mayfair estate agent Edward Erdman, who asked him if Trafalgar, the owners of Cunard with its ships and hotels (including the Bristol opposite the Ritz) would like to buy the Ritz Hotel (London) Ltd. Broackes's first reaction was to ask why Erdman had come to Trafalgar when there were at least two well-known hoteliers whom he must have thought of first – Sir Charles Forte and Maxwell Joseph; the answer was that neither of them was buying anything for the time being. Erdman made it clear to Broackes that as the Ritz was a public company, with major shareholders not necessarily unanimous in their desire to sell, it was not possible to be sure what price, if any, would be acceptable; though the agent had received indications that £1.8 million would do the trick. Trafalgar offered what was asked,

A store-room in the basement during the hotel's redecoration
(now part of the Casino).

but no clear answer came back and, as Nigel Broackes says in his amiable autobiography, *A Growing Concern*, 'the matter dragged on indecisively for the rest of the year.' Sir Charles Clore seems to have been rather an obstruction on the Ritz side; he 'behaved as if he owned the place, which he did not', says Broackes.

By the beginning of 1976 the transaction seemed to Broackes to have 'petered out'. The Trafalgar chairman was disappointed about this because, though he regarded the food as mediocre, the 'staff never changed and the ambience was enchanting – to me, *la belle époque.*' He felt:

> One of the attractions of the Ritz was that it had never been modernized. Most hotels, in seventy years would have been 'done over' two or three times, and any original charm would have disappeared beyond recall, as one contemporary style after another had been applied in successive layers of current tastes in decor. But this one, particularly as far as the ground floor was concerned, was a magnificent, original artefact, needing only to be restored. What a pity, I thought: the Ritz Company had not the resources in talent or cash to carry out the work; we were uniquely qualified with Trollope & Colls, to do the job; and reasonably qualified to run the hotel; but it seemed that this was not to be.

However, just over a year after Trafalgar's chairman had found an oyster at the Ritz, the deputy chairman landed a far bigger catch: the beautiful old dowager of Piccadilly herself. Victor Matthews was lunching in the Restaurant at his favourite table, No. 29, and while he was in the hotel happened to run into Geoffrey Grahame, the manager. 'I told him of my disappointment that our offer had been turned down', remembers Matthews, 'but he said that it might be worth another try.'

'One moment', said Grahame. 'Have you ever met Sir Guy? He is sitting over there.' In the Palm Court (or Winter Garden as it was originally called) there indeed sat the forlorn figure of Sir Guy Bracewell Smith, chairman of the Ritz, who had recently lost his American wife and was himself to die later that year.

'Within half an hour,' says Matthews, 'I had committed myself to buying the Ritz. I decided to go ahead unilaterally, whatever happened, as this was the snip of all time – the site alone was obviously worth £2.7

The gilt is restored.

Renovating the marbling (*above*);
and (*right*) the dining room of the Casino.

The striking triangular staircase near the south-west corner of the hotel (*above*); and the *trompe l'oeil* ceiling of the Restaurant (*right*). Garlands based on 'Le bal paré et masqué'.

Bronze garlands and chandeliers reflected in the Restaurant's great mirror of bevelled glass (*left*); and (*above*) the 'Alice in Wonderland' door.

The Ritz Casino: over 6,000 books of gold leaf were used.

million in cash that was paid for it. It was such a bargain that in fact I was prepared to raise the money myself if necessary – that is if the board of Trafalgar didn't back me. I didn't think that the board would be all that keen and, quite frankly, I was even rather looking forward to being the proprietor myself – perhaps a little disappointed when they did decide to back me!'

The deal was completed on 26 March 1976 and on the same day Victor Matthews reassured one of the hotel's *habitués*, Patrick Sergeant, City Editor of the *Daily Mail*: 'Nobody need fear we will do anything to damage the Ritz's prestige. We are buying it for its great name and its great reputation. The Ritz is losing about £3,000 a week. Our target is to bring it into profit next year, and to go on from there. To do that we will have to spend something like £2 million on refurbishing. There will be new plumbing, rewiring, and an extra 40 or 50 beds to raise capacity to 180 or 200. At the moment the Ritz is less than half full. We mean to improve occupancy to 70 or 80 per cent. We can do that by linking the Ritz to our general promotion of the *QE2* and our other hotels. The main problem with the Ritz is that it is too small to be successfully independent. We can give it marketing, centralized purchasing and even the use of the car park over the road at our Bristol Hotel'. Before long the micro-chip was added to the benefits that Cunard Hotels brought its new flagship: at a cost of just under £20,000, a computer system was installed to facilitate advance reservations, more detailed guests' accounts, checks on vacancies and so on. Staff redundancies were definitely ruled out however, and only two senior members of staff left after the takeover.

The staff at the Ritz had always enjoyed a reputation for individuality. The eccentrics in the past had included 'Mad Norman', who used to peel potatoes in the early hours of the morning wearing a copy of an Inca headdress and then spend the rest of the day busking locally; 'The Blotting Paper Man', who spent a large proportion of his time tearing small pieces of blotting paper into small strips which he then balanced on his nose and blew off one at a time as he stalked along the corridors; Pierre, the waiter, who failed to take up the traditional tumbler of whisky from the storeman to the hotel secretary on his birthday, but drank it instead (both he and 'The Blotting Paper Man' were sacked, of course); and Paddy, the bin man, whose house overlooking his beloved Stamford Bridge football ground was full of unopened pay packets dating back to 1919 – 'I rather got the feeling that if I held on to them they might be worth something one day.' The personnel included in the takeover also numbered Tiger, the Ritz cat, whose diet of caviar and smoked salmon has led to the necessity of an annual slimming cure in Belgravia; Tiger is a keen television viewer in the boiler room, being particularly partial to *Coronation Street* and *News at Ten* before retiring.

Peregrine Worsthorne may have waxed nostalgic about 'that half-tipsy old cloakroom attendant in an uncreased uniform with egg down his front' and 'the fat waiter whose trousers and waistcoat never met', but Victor Matthews was unimpressed by the 'grease stains on the waiters' suits'. When he addressed the staff after the takeover and was asked the inevitable question about pay, he replied: 'There's no more money for the time being, but you can all have a new suit.' Matthews recalls: 'I was determined first of all to lift their morale. These new suits did a lot for their pride; the service improved out of all recognition and I'm happy to say we've kept almost all the same people – it's just now they're a different bunch of characters.'

'The place was in a pretty sorry state when we took over', says Matthews. 'The curtains were falling apart, the carpets had holes in them . . .' Nigel Broackes helped his old colleague choose the new carpet for the Winter Garden (as the chairman prefers to call the Palm Court):

> At eleven one morning the furniture was removed, and one carpet after another was spread out before us; it was surprising what a variety of forty and fifty-foot long carpets were instantly available in London. There was one which we both liked and I asked the price.
> 'Fourteen thousand pounds, Sir!'
> 'Offer him twelve,' said Victor, and we left.

It was Victor Matthews who masterminded the redecoration of the hotel. 'Being an old hand at the building game,' he says, 'I decided to take personal responsibility for the design and hired the architects and designers. It was the sort of challenge I enjoy – we went through the whole thing: carpets, chairs, the lot. Of course we were in a special position through owning Trollope & Colls who are virtually the only people now capable of doing such a luxury job, what with gold and silver leaf and so forth. I took a personal hand in everything and worked closely with the painting manager, Bill Beasley, sorting out the colours. I wanted

The Prime Minister, Margaret Thatcher, with Victor Matthews, Deputy Chairman of Trafalgar House, at the Ritz for the dinner in honour of Sir John Junor, Editor of the *Sunday Express*.

to interpret the best of the old while also giving the Ritz the best of the new. The old lifts were replaced and we put in another new lift; all sorts of modern improvements were made. I thought there were too many "lost leaders" in the old huge bedrooms and it was time to catch up; so I got several different designers to create the new concept at the Ritz of the smaller bedsitting room. This meant that we now had 166 rooms instead of about 100.'

The hotel's works manager, Bill Martin, recalls that Victor Matthews was at the Ritz almost every day as the enormous job of redecoration got under way. One of the biggest problems, Martin says, was 'to keep the building operative during the refurbishment. The boilers were extinct and we couldn't put new boilers in and still keep the place operative so we had to get permission from Westminster City Council to put a couple of boilers out on the pavement with hoardings around them and generate steam while new boilers were being installed.' The rewiring was also a major headache; it is usual to work on one floor at a time when redecorating a place like the Ritz, but that really only applies to the actual decorating rather than plumbing or rewiring. 'Plumbing systems are vertical,' explains Martin. 'So it was difficult to carry out a project vertically and still leave access along all the corridors and get building materials to these rooms. Hoists were erected outside to bring material in through the windows. As the Ritz is a listed building we weren't allowed to alter the structure at all during the redecorating. There was difficulty with double-glazing the windows because we couldn't alter the outside of the structure. The windows are now eight to ten inches thick.'

The space that Mewès and Davis allowed themselves to build the hotel made it possible for today's architects and designers to find room for more bedrooms. Corridors in the suites have been incorporated into the bedrooms, which have been redesigned to make use of the available space. The front bedrooms have been furnished in a recognizable 'Ritz' style; those at the rear tend to be more modern. Six designers were given the chance to create six suites each; all were different. The seventh floor, once comprising staff accommodation, was converted into guest bedrooms and there is now a separate staff hostel. The design of all the bedrooms in the hotel takes full advantage of the original marble fireplaces – still in magnificent condition – and much of the fine original furniture is being restored and maintained. All the bathrooms, to the regret of many traditionalists among the old clients, are modern.

Because of the plumbing problems explained by Bill Martin, 'stacks' of rooms had to be renovated at the same time which meant the inconvenience of having builders on every floor. At one stage there were 350 builders on site and Lord Clark's sage observation about the Ritz 'being the only hotel left with an atmosphere of calm sanity' was, temporarily at least, open to disagreement. In the thick of the redecoration programme only 36 bedrooms were available, but their occupants and the staff coped with great fortitude. 'Clients at the Ritz', said Grahame (the manager who smoothly saw the hotel through these upheavals), 'are extremely loyal and very constructive' – they criticized some of the rooms in a positive manner which helped in the design of others. Grahame himself slept in about thirty of the rooms to make sure they 'worked'.

The clients' loyalty was put to some quite severe tests in the 1970s because, apart from the renovations inside, there was also the building of the new underground line at Green Park right next to the Ritz which, as a regular American visitor recalls, led to 'twenty-four hours a day of pneumatic jackhammers, floodlighting at night and other horrors ... but it's our London "home" and we wouldn't have given that up easily.' This gentleman was pleased with the new bathrooms, the televisions and the fact that he and his wife were no longer at risk of falling flat on their faces over the ever-widening holes in the carpets; 'a great boon is that you can now dial direct out on automatic STD telephones – that business of

Apart from the renovation of the hotel itself, Ritz patrons of the late 1970s had to suffer the building of the new underground line at Green Park.

holding on while the operator got your number didn't have much charm.'

The King and Queen of Sweden were fully understanding and patient when their breakfast – which a waiter was bringing along the corridor to their suite – became engulfed in a cascade of bricks and mortar disgorged by a lift and the manager explained that breakfast would be a little late that morning.

The glorious high-ceilinged Restaurant was carefully restored, though Quentin Crewe recalls one of the Italian waiters telling him he was disappointed with the way the marble pillars were cleaned. 'In Carrara we have zee special stuff to clean zee pillars,' he said plaintively, 'but here we clean zeese lovely pillars with *Ajax*.' One of Crewe's successors as restaurant critic of *Harpers & Queen*, Gaia Servadio, said she felt 'like a Richard Strauss heroine' having lunch 'under pale blue Boucher-like clouds festooned with golden chandeliers, a symphony of pinks everywhere.' She was 'delighted to see that the Ritz Restaurant, under new management, has much improved, not only in the service which was welcoming and prompt, but in the actual quality of the food.' The Chef des Cuisines, Jacques Viney, who joined the Ritz in 1958 from the Jardin des Gourmets having previously worked at the Dorchester, feels that the Ritz kitchens had 'got into a bit of a rut under M. Avignon who'd been there donkey's years', but honoured four of the hotel's past chefs – Malley, Limasseau, Herbodeau and Avignon – in a gourmet festival at which he recreated the menus of his predecessors for the Restaurant. The wine cellar had become very run down under the previous owners and Harry Waugh, chairman of the Wine Society, was commissioned 'to produce the finest wine list possible', forming a tasting panel which now consists of Nick Vecchione (Cunard Hotels' managing director), Martin Delahay (the wine buyer for Cunard) and Alastair Nugent. As well as an excellent choice of French vintages, the new list includes some of the best wines from California and Australia. An innovation in the Restaurant is what Barbara Leigh Evans, the Ritz's public relations lady, describes as 'gentle music' provided by the Norman Percival Trio (who have recorded an album called *Puttin' on the Ritz*).

Some people were rather shocked by the introduction of shops under the arcade in Piccadilly but, as is often the case in these matters, they were showing their historical ignorance. The Rue de Rivoli in Paris, which provided the model for the Ritz arcade, has always had shops, and originally at the London Ritz Robert Green, the florists and greengrocers, occupied the space later converted into the Rivoli Bar and now once more used for shops. Trafalgar decided to exploit this neglected opportunity and let the shops for £80,000 a year; as Nigel Broackes points out, they 'do not intrude at all within the ground floor'.

Even more controversially, the old Grill Room was let to Maxwell Joseph of the Grand Metropolitan group at £180,000 per annum for use as a casino. Here again, though, those ready to denigrate the new owners of the Ritz were wide of the mark. 'The new casino will abound with all the elegance and style of Edwardian rococo, much more so than the Grill Room and Bar used to do', wrote Peregrine Worsthorne. 'For in fact those favourite rooms of Aly Khan and Evelyn Waugh were a rather ugly 1930s addition, carved out of César Ritz's original ballroom which is now being recreated exactly as it was before the First World War.' Joseph and his company spent a million pounds (with a Trafalgar subsidiary) on restoring the basement; the designer was Robert Lush, of the Richmond Design Group, who restored the Café de la Paix to the satisfaction of the French Ministry of Arts and whose plans for the Ritz Casino won the approval of the GLC's Surveyor of Historical Buildings whose consent was required in every detail. No expense was spared: over 6,000 books of gold leaf were used and Julia Stubbs, one of the painters who applied the £21,000 worth of gold to cover the decorations, says she had to be careful not to sneeze.

'I suppose it isn't worse than a discotheque, is it?' said actor James Mason on the opening night of the Ritz Casino. Before the gaming started, Baron Henri de Montesquieu, one of a family that César Ritz himself often served in *la belle époque* and a director of Moet & Chandon, performed the perilous champagne cascade – slicing the tops off champagne bottles with a sabre, thus filling 500 champagne glasses arranged in a cone or ziggurat. The five hundred who drank the stuff included Sir Charles Clore, Jimmy Hill, Fiona Richmond (fully clothed), Larry Adler and two ladies more often seen upstairs, Olga Deterding and Lady Diana Cooper (whose maid is married to the Casino doorman, Eduardo).

Lady Diana still loves going to the beautiful Restaurant whether to have a meal or see one of the Japanese dressmaker Yuki's fashion shows. When Ian Fleming's widow Ann asked Lady Diana to a party for Patrick Leigh Fermor at the Ritz, the doyenne of the hotel's clients 'thought it would be a small dinner for six, but when I got there I found it was for a hundred people. Paddy, of course, is a wonderful character. His idea of fun is to sing *Uncle Tom Cobbley* in Greek or *Hearts of Oak* in Hindustani. There were five tables and such delicious chat. It must have been the first party like that for five years.'

The Ritz's distinctive clients from an earlier age still came to stay: the Earl of Carnarvon, Viscount Head, Sir Harold Acton. The late Viva King's annual party for the Royal Academy's Private View Day was succeeded by the lunch given for 'excellent raconteurs and beautiful women' by Margaret Rawlings, the actress (Lady Barlow); her guests included Dame Rebecca West.

Jacqueline Onassis frequently stays at the Ritz when she is in London; once, when asked if everything was 'all right' by the hotel's housekeeper, Kate Clifford, the former First Lady replied: 'It's like paradise.' Shortly before the takeover Mrs Onassis and Hugh Fraser, the Tory politician who had escorted her back to the Ritz after a dinner out, were observed banging on the locked door. An eye witness told the *Daily Mirror*: 'It was several minutes before the door was unlocked. Jackie [*sic*] said she was cold – she only had on a velvet suit and it was snowing.' A hotel spokesman reassured the *Mirror's* reporter that 'there was no trouble and she was quite happy about things when I let her in.' Helmut Newton, the photographer, was less happy at finding himself locked out of the Ritz recently when he returned at one in the morning and had difficulty in gaining admittance.

Faithful clients of the hotel include Jacqueline Onassis and Graham Greene.

A memorable moment of the 1970s at the Ritz was the sight of the Prince of Wales dancing on top of the piano with the pop-singer Elton John at a private party in the Marie Antoinette suite. Geoffrey Grahame, who retired in the autumn of 1979, remembers having to gently persuade another pop-singer who went down to see the hall porter in his stockinged feet that 'you really do not do that sort of thing in the Ritz'.

The Marie Antoinette suite tends to be used more for business functions these days. The Square Mile Club dines there, and the Marquess of Tavistock remembers being very impressed with Shaikh Yamani's handling of questions from members when this crucial figure in oil came as the guest of Henry Keswick, proprietor of the *Spectator*. The tradition of holding Election parties at the Ritz was carried on by Express Newspapers in 1979; the *Daily Express*, of course, is now owned by Trafalgar House and Victor Matthews also launched his new *Daily Star* at the hotel. Fleet Street's longest-serving editor, Sir John Junor of the *Sunday Express*, was given a 25th anniversary party at the Ritz and addressed the gathering which included the Prime Minister, Mrs Thatcher (herself a Ritz regular, favouring table No. 6 in the Restaurant). 'You can sell newspapers for a time on big, beautiful boobs and bottoms,' the formidable Scotsman told them, 'but someone is going to come along with bigger ones and there is no permanency in it.' The *Tatler* (another publication in which Trafalgar House until recently had a stake) celebrated its 270th anniversary at the Ritz with such luminaries present as David Frost, Janet Street-Porter, Lady Rothermere, Dai Llewellyn, Joan Collins (described by one of the waiters as the most beautiful woman he had ever seen), Reginald Bosanquet, as well as the magazine's witty editor Tina Brown and her diarist Margaret Duchess of Argyll.

One of the guests, Alastair Forbes, once said that he was sorry the Ritz had 'become a waystation on package-cruise-trips with teatime rendezvous spoiled by tartan-trousered tourists ex-USA'; but the *Daily Telegraph*'s Elisabeth de Stroumillo found her room 'just right: not awesomely large or over-opulent but big enough for a sofa and a couple of armchairs (plus the inevitable TV), and decorated in the best English town-house tradition. It took a measure of willpower to emerge ...' Just two years after the takeover Egon Ronay made the Ritz his 'Hotel of the Year', saying that the hotel 'once again lives up to its founder's name and no effort and expense have been spared to complete its restoration and modernization.'

The Marie Antoinette private dining room.

CHAPTER

VIII

THE RITZ TODAY

'Creep in under the low concrete ceiling of a modern hotel', wrote Peter Fleetwood-Hesketh. 'In the minutes before your intrusion is acknowledged you can study the drab decor, resembling an old provincial airport. At last a lowered head is raised. "Yes?" it asks, to which your answer should be "No."'

At the Ritz, however, 'the moment you enter, beaming faces on every side make you feel you have come home. Even the younger looking ones have been there perhaps ten, perhaps fifteen years, others thirty or more. You pay no more for this human reception than for lack of it elsewhere.'

Lord Mountbatten said that one 'could always tell the people who belonged at the Ritz by whether they used the posh entrance in Piccadilly or the (proper) entrance in Arlington Street'; so entering by the latter up the steps, through the swing doors, we are faced on our right by the hall porter's desk. Here Victor Legg presides. Victor joined the Ritz in 1935 and took over as head porter from George when he retired in 1961: 'I'm a relic of the time when they'd come and stay three months for the season and then the Royal Family would leave London in August and everybody blew', he says. 'Then they went up shooting and London was empty; then they all came back – a more ordered existence. People had servants; half the single rooms here now were once servants' rooms.'

Victor has adapted to the modern world with great good humour: 'Mick Jagger comes here – no trouble at all; Charlie Watts comes here – he's one of the nicest men that comes here, very quiet, no bother at all . . . you've got to move with the times; in the snobbish old days, you could tell a person by their dress, but you can't do that now.' A hall porter, says Victor, 'should know about everything from a safety pin to a battleship.' 'If you like people, it's the game to be in . . . It's also a great challenge to

The appeal to the eye in the Restaurant.

the ego. You do your best and say nothing's impossible, you're going to do it. You're more or less like a father confessor ... the charm of it – and sometimes the annoyance of it – is that you can pick up the phone and you don't know what's at the other end.' Raymond Guest, the American racehorse owner, former Ambassador to Ireland and nephew of the 1st Viscount Wimborne, once rang Victor and asked him to 'buy me a helicopter'; on another occasion one of the American Astors rang to say 'I'm dissatisfied with my tailor. Find me a tailor and he can fly over here and make me some suits.' Victor duly obliged. Graham Greene is a particular favourite with Victor; Greene wrote him a poem in which the jokes include a reference to a certain wine which should be drunk when it's young, not old, but it took so long for the waiter to bring it up ... The refrain of the ballad, composed while the writer was suffering the renovations in the Ritz, goes:

'But in a hotel where Victor ceased to rule I would not wish to be.'

Lord Tavistock, whom Victor used to make a fuss of when he was a baby, is very attached to hall porters: 'They're immensely powerful operators – get extraordinary things done for you. I'm very proud to be a member of their marvellous organization, the Society of Golden Keys (*Clefs d'Or*); it literally opens doors for you all over the world.'

Opposite the hall porter's desk is the reception area. Philip Truelove, who is in charge of 'Front Office Services', says that 'a card is kept on each client on which we make notes of any special preferences they might have – if they like a cup of tea on arrival, if they like a certain newspaper, if they like to be called at a certain time.' All the receptionists speak at least one foreign language; the first female receptionist, benefiting from the Equal Opportunities Act, joined the Ritz in 1979. Jayne Harrison, who used to work at the Waldorf, now handles the advance reservations at the Ritz. She says that about 30 per cent of those staying the night at the hotel are new arrivals that day; overall roughly 40 per cent of the guests today are Americans and a similar percentage are British, with perhaps half of the latter being businessmen whose companies are footing the bill. Philip Truelove recalls the time an American couple came in to have a look round:

'Gee, has this hotel always been a hotel?' the man asked Truelove.

'Yes, sir, it's always been just as you see it now.'

'Gee, honey,' the American said to his wife, 'I thought it used to be a railway station.'

'You can pick up the 'phone and you don't know what's at the other end': Victor Legg, the hall porter, at his station.

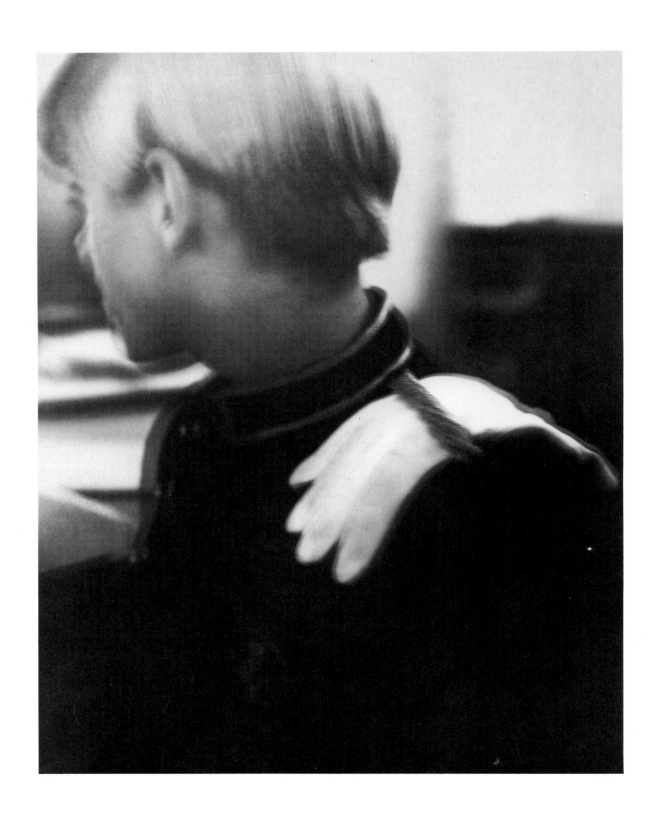

The original page boys' uniform (*above*).
Right The Ritz Hotel 'club': London manager Jack Hudson (*centre*) with the managers of the 'other Ritzes'.

Behind the reception area is the manager's office which faces on to Arlington Street. Jack Hudson, who succeeded Geoffrey Grahame as manager in 1979, began in the hotel industry as a page boy at the Savoy in 1930. After wartime service in the RAF he returned to the Savoy for sixteen years before becoming front manager at the Mandarin Hotel in Hong Kong; he was then successively house manager of the Café Royal, chief executive of the Motel International de Lyon and executive director of Cartiers in Hong Kong before joining Trafalgar House in 1968. For Cunard Trafalgar he has managed hotels in the Caribbean and became manager of the Hotel Bristol in 1975. He works closely with Nick Vecchione, Cunard Hotels' managing director, whose office overlooks the Ritz and who takes a passionate interest in his flagship and its history. A dapper, dedicated man, Hudson is keenly aware of the demands of the new type of Ritz client, the top executive. He talks enthusiastically about the setting up of a Club of Ritz Hotels – Madrid, Lisbon, Barcelona and Boston are the 'other Ritzes' which recognize each other, as well as the original in Paris (now largely owned by an Arab consortium). This would help promote the name 'Ritz' all over the world and Hudson mentions discreet Ritz crests being considered for ties, headscarves, etc.

Jack Hudson's deputy is Malcolm Allcock, formerly house manager of the RAF Club in Piccadilly, who is mainly concerned with personnel and administrative work. 'In the old days,' says Allcock, 'there were 240–250 staff; now it's 220 and the summer payroll is 260. The staff turnover is about average in positions like chambermaids and *commis* waiters – obviously a lot of them are working here to get the reputation of having worked at the Ritz and then they'll move on. Senior staff tend to stay – thirteen of the staff have 20 years, or more, of service; 60 per cent of the staff are English.'

We then walk along the corridor towards the Palm Court (or Winter Garden). It is time for tea:

> Under the ornate gilt and glass ceiling in the pale pink and cream lounge, seated on comfortable pink velvet chairs and sofas and with gold cherubs looking on, tea at the Ritz is, thank goodness, still magical. The china is white and pale blue, pretty but surprisingly rather modern. Delicate fingers of white bread and butter are striped appropriately with pale pink ham, pale peach [the tint now given to the glass in the ceiling, incidentally] smoked salmon, cream cheese, pale green cucumber. Cakes are delectable: tiny éclairs, fresh fruit tarts, plain chocolate sauces and a huge central gateau with fresh strawberries, cream and the lightest sponge. The atmosphere is totally relaxed, conversation from the intriguing mixture of guests is quiet but not self-conscious and the service is immaculate. [Evelyn Grubb, *Harpers & Queen*, January 1980]

The immaculate service was, of course, supervised by someone described by the late Maurice Richardson as 'an Irishman of genius', Michael Twomey, from Fermoy, County Cork, who joined the Ritz in 1946. Looking incredibly young and, in Patrick Leigh Fermor's view, 'exactly like Benjamin Britten', Michael retains that slightly ironic Irish lilt which blends so well with his attentive yet never servile air. Peter Quennell says: 'He was always so fond of my son, let him exercise trains across the floor and helped him feed the goldfish in the marble fountain. He was also kind to my dog; and although dogs were supposed to be forbidden access, let him sit on Saturday mornings behind my chair.' When Michael's own son was studying for his O-levels, Quennell would bring along copies of his

Michael Twomey, the 'Irish prince of the Ritz', adjusts his bow-tie on the steps of his kingdom, the Palm Court.

'The spacious but rather severe entrance corridor' leading to the Restaurant.

magazine *History Today*. This 'Irish prince of the Ritz' is delightfully sympathetic and gentle, as well as being a diplomatist. Cyril Connolly and Evelyn Waugh, not the easiest of customers, are remembered with understanding. Of the irascible Waugh Michael says there was 'no harm in him, really. He didn't mean it. It was just his way . . .' Michael knows and admits that the Ritz 'got away under the guise of faded splendour for many years', but all is well now and he is happier than ever. 'If I was not at the Ritz today,' he says, 'I would be out of catering.' Malcolm Muggeridge once said that he found the atmosphere of tea at the Ritz 'both calm and polite. It is undoubtedly my favourite meal of the day.' One eccentric regular in the Palm Court mixes tea with coffee in the same cup.

As for cocktails there, dry martini is the most popular drink with Americans, says Michael, but champagne, whether alone or as Buck's Fizz, is universally in demand. The hotel's own cocktail is called 'Ricky' and includes such items as lime and gum syrup. Michael has a staff of five serving tea and cocktails with him.

Back down the two steps of the Palm Court, turn left and carry on down the corridor. As Peter Fleetwood-Hesketh says, 'it is always a pleasure to move through the spacious but rather severe entrance corridor into the great Restaurant whose sumptuous elegance is enhanced by the contrast; or into the charming Marie Antoinette room adjoining, used for private parties.'

Marcel Hoeffler, the Restaurant manager, a neat bronzed figure, is assisted by Luís Martin, formerly at the Ritzes in Barcelona and Madrid. Luís (or Martin as he is known) shows his watch which was given to him by the Prime Minister of Malaysia; Orson Welles once gave him a cigar so huge that it took the Spaniard 2 hours and 47 minutes to smoke. He reminisces about some of the famous guests he has served in the twenty-seven years he has worked at the Ritz – The Queen Mother, Prince Philip, Princess Margaret, Emperor Haile Sellassie, Sophia Loren, Deborah Kerr, Rita Hayworth, Gene Kelly. The senior head waiter, Alphonso Styranau, has noticed an encouraging increase in the Restaurant's evening business. 'Ten years ago business was slack – there would be a maximum of six or perhaps ten *couverts*; now we have thirty or forty *couverts*.' His philosophy is that, whoever they are, 'every customer is the same – and I try to be kind and nice to all of them (even if they will drink red wine with fish!).' Vincent Devivo has been a waiter at the Ritz for over fifty years: 'Nothing's changed much really; same table-cloths, same cutlery; glasses

The light from Green Park (*above*).
Luigi, the wine waiter (*right*).

are the same with the crest on, same carpet, same chairs ...' He has always had the same station, for breakfast and lunch, on the left as you go in by the statue of Neptune.

Jacques Viney, the chef, a tall, quietly amusing Frenchman, describes himself as 'a bit of a dreamer'. He takes a keen interest in the history of food from Egyptian and Roman times onwards, quoting Chansonnier on Bacchus. Always jotting down notes, he hopes to write it all up one day in a book which will have the 'lid off'. The chef works a twelve-hour day, beginning with the ordering of food from the markets in the dawn hours. He remembers Nubar Gulbenkian as one of his most colourful patrons; unlike his father, Nubar was very happy to avail himself of the hotel's own cuisine and his favourite dish was *Canard Montmorency* (duck with black cherries, foie gras and truffles). Having survived the vicissitudes of the Ritz for twenty years, Viney was justly proud of the Ronay award in 1978.

The wine waiter, Luigi, has one assistant and two *commis* waiters; they collect from the dispense bar which carries between three to six bottles of everything there is in the wine cellar, including the Ritz's noted vintage ports. The cellarman is Drago Marinov, originally a chemical engineer in Bulgaria, who came to England in 1972. He remembers the restocking of the cellar in 1976 under the supervision of Harry Waugh as a great experience: 'We tasted over one thousand wines; it will never be repeated on the same scale.'

The rotunda (*above*); and (*right*) part of a suite seen through a looking-glass.

The bed linen is changed every day (*above*).
Ritz insisted on brass beds as more hygienic than wooden ones (*right*).

Upstairs by the splendid rotunda staircase – or the lifts – one can get one's hair cut at Maurice Vian's salon on the first floor. During the war Vian, then in Knightsbridge, was in trouble for being an alien, but his customers in high places were able to help him out. In the old days there used to be a ladies' hairdresser; at one stage it was run by a Mrs Kemp-Welch (a connexion by marriage of the lady who writes 'Jennifer's Diary' in *Harpers & Queen*).

The bedrooms are under the supervision of Kate Clifford, the executive housekeeper, who has been at the Ritz for seven years; previously she was cashier at the Waldorf. She is responsible for some fifty staff – housekeepers, valets, chambermaids, porters, linen workers. Outside laundries are used for the bed linen (Egyptian cotton, changed every day; towels are changed twice a day) and the guests' clothes. There are usually nineteen maids on duty on a normal day. 'What I like about the Ritz is the nice crowd of people', says Miss Clifford. 'The Ritz has been kind to me and good for me. It has a very grand image, but it is friendly. People come here because it's exclusive and quiet. You get very few complaints.'

May Jones has been a chambermaid at the Ritz for forty years and remembers the time when the bedrooms 'used to have log fires. The valets would bring up the logs and we'd set the fires and light them so they'd be going when the guests woke up.' She misses living in the hotel herself: 'I loved it . . . but it was needing a little paint.' She adds, 'I'm glad they've kept the kidney-shaped dressing tables and the tallboys.' May reminisces about the war, private servants ('nobody brings a man now, except perhaps Loel Guinness'), Suzi Voltaire, the Astaires, Ambassador Biddle, Piccadilly as it used to be ... 'everybody going out in evening dress'. She says she's 'always been happy here; I never got fed up. Everyone is like a friend to you.'

The seventeen maintenance staff – electricians, boiler engineers, painters, carpenters, upholsterers – work under Bill Martin, whose own connexion with the Ritz goes back to 1947 when he was called in by his predecessor, Mr Worrall, as an electrical engineer. 'The maintenance system goes on until 11 o'clock at night', says Martin. 'You have to be there in case somebody might have an American hairdryer and you've got to change the plug for them.' He is 'very happy with the way the Ritz has been restored to its former grandeur. It was gradually running down. A lot of the services were in lead and had metal fatigue. Of course they weren't charging enough before the takeover, but then it had run down so much that, frankly, it wouldn't have been worth it.' The works manager sees it as 'a constant challenge to work here because when anything, even the smallest thing, has to be replaced, it must be chosen with care to conform. The wall plugs, the electric fires, the radios and so on all have to be made specially for us.'

The Ritz conjures up various images. Mrs Amber Lightfoot Walker from New York feels 'that something wonderfully illicit should happen to me at the Ritz ... a man with a great moustache smoking a fat cigar, rather an Edwardian figure I now see, should appear and attempt to seduce me – it was the right setting!' (Not the ghost of César Ritz surely? *Not* at the Ritz, madam.) For Esther Rantzen the Ritz is the last word in glamour. For Peter Fleetwood-Hesketh and 'those who dislike change, the Ritz is a haven and a refuge. Those excellent people who so courteously attend to one's needs remain there year after year, and this continuity helps to maintain the atmosphere of homeliness regrettably absent from so many modern establishments.' For Lord Tavistock, the Ritz 'has a wonderful atmosphere – friendly and yet rather awe-inspiring; everybody is excited to go to the Ritz'; and Patrick Leigh Fermor has 'always loved it – it seems quite unlike other hotels in character and atmosphere, as different, in its way, as the Cavendish used to be.' Anthony Blond finds it 'a surprisingly egalitarian place: Gulbenkian and everyone else have always been equal there'. Fleur Cowles, who once administered a cure for Blond's dysentery over the table in the Restaurant having sent out for

A leonine corner of the roof.

some Lomatol, says that 'it is still far from a Texas cowboy stop-over . . . I love beauty and the Ritz is beautiful. The surroundings are wonderful. I feel loyal to the place. You have to keep coming back – it deserves it.'

Victor Matthews loves the place too. 'We're now offering more of a family approach; this means that the children will carry on coming when they grow up. All right, we may have lost some of the old clientele but then the old aristocracy has tended to disappear from the Ritz anyway. We've got this *QE2* package deal tied in with the Ritz and the dear old ship advertises the hotel all over the world. We get a lot more people from overseas now. Nowhere else has the same prestige; the Ritz is still out on its own.

'Looking to the future, I'd like to introduce one or two really *de luxe* "Presidential" suites – rather like the special suites we've put on the *QE2*. I'm thinking of attracting the really important people, like Heads of State.'

Whatever happens in the future, one can confidently predict, as this marvel of Edwardian opulence prepares to celebrate its – or can we say 'her' – seventy-fifth birthday, that the London Ritz will continue to fulfil César Ritz's proud dream that the hotel should embody 'the highest developments of artistic comfort in the twentieth century'.

INDEX

SOURCES OF ILLUSTRATIONS

The photographs reproduced in this book
were kindly supplied by:
BBC Hulton Picture Library, 11, 14, 23, 26,
    28, 29, 30, 56, 57, 62, 65, 72, 76, 77,
    80, 83, 85, 86, 92, 98, 100, 102, 138
Bibliothèque Nationale, Paris, 15
Keith Collie, 2, 33, 34/5, 36/7, 38, 39,
    40, 41, 50, 52, 53, 54, 61, 91, 118, 123,
    150, 156/7, 158/9, 160, 171, 172, 175,
    176, 179, 180, 182, 183, 184, 185, 186,
    187, 189, 191
The Daily Telegraph Colour Library, 149
Mary Evans Picture Library, 21, 138
Courtesy Mrs Hewitt, 94, 97
Steve Johnston, 144
Keystone Press Agency, 108, 123, 126
Mander and Mitchenson Theatre Collection,
    86, 99
The Mansell Collection, 66, 71, 78
Musée Carnavalet, Paris, 21
Popperfoto, 82, 85, 98, 108/9, 119, 124,
    127, 131, 134, 138/9
Rex Features, 143, 168
The Ritz, 9, 29, 37, 44, 51, 76, 130, 153,
    154/5, 162, 165, 177
Sotheby Belgravia, 114, 126
The Marquess of Tavistock, 104
John Topham Picture Library, 19, 86, 108,
    120, 133, 134, 169